Unit Resource Guide
Unit 16

Assessing Our Learning

THIRD EDITION

KENDALL/HUNT PUBLISHING COMPANY
4050 Westmark Drive   Dubuque, Iowa 52002

A TIMS® Curriculum
University of Illinois at Chicago

UIC The University of Illinois
at Chicago

The original edition was based on work supported by the National Science Foundation under grant No. MDR 9050226 and the University of Illinois at Chicago. Any opinions, findings, and conclusions or recommendations expressed in this publication are those of the author(s) and do not necessarily reflect the views of the granting agencies.

Letter Home

Assessing Our Learning

Date: _____

Dear Family Member:

The final unit of fourth grade provides opportunities to reflect on your child's growth in mathematics. By comparing work completed near the beginning of the school year with work completed in the middle and at the end, you will see the progress your child has made. We hope you will note big improvements not only with math skills and content, but also with your child's ability to solve sophisticated problems and communicate his or her ideas.

As part of the assessment activities in this unit, your child will take a test on the division facts. Please help your child review for this test with the *Triangle Flash Cards*.

An imaginary town of ants provides the setting for an investigation of length, area, and width.

As we work on activities in school, you can help at home by:

- Encouraging your child to think about and discuss the skills and concepts he or she has learned this year in mathematics class.
- Offering your child an opportunity to share with you the work collected in his or her portfolio.
- Asking your child to tell about his or her favorite labs or other math activities completed this year.

Thank you for all your help and support.

Sincerely,

_____

Carta al hogar

Evaluando lo que hemos aprendido

Fecha: _____

Estimado miembro de familia:

La unidad final de cuarto grado ofrece oportunidades para reflexionar sobre el avance de su hijo/a en las matemáticas. Al comparar el trabajo completado a comienzos del año escolar con el trabajo completado a mitad del año y al final, usted podrá ver el avance que ha hecho su hijo/a. Esperamos que usted observe grandes avances no sólo en las destrezas y los contenidos matemáticos, sino también en la habilidad de su hijo/a para resolver problemas sofisticados y comunicar sus ideas.

Una investigación sobre la longitud, el área y el ancho transcurre en una ciudad imaginaria habitada por hormigas.

Como parte de la evaluación de las actividades de esta unidad, su hijo/a tomará un examen sobre las tablas de división. Ayude a su hijo/a a repasar para este examen usando las tarjetas triangulares.

A medida que trabajamos en actividades de la escuela, usted puede ayudar en casa haciendo lo siguiente:

- Anime a su hijo/a a pensar y hablar acerca de las destrezas y los conceptos que aprendió durante el año en la clase de matemáticas.
- Dé a su hijo/a la oportunidad de compartir con usted el trabajo guardado en su portafolio.
- Pídale a su hijo/a que le cuente cuáles fueron sus investigaciones u otras actividades de matemáticas preferidas que completó durante el año.

Gracias por toda su ayuda y su apoyo.

Atentamente,

_____

Table of Contents

Unit 16
Assessing Our Learning

Unit 16

Outline
Assessing Our Learning

Unit Summary

Estimated Class Sessions 9-11

This unit reviews, extends, and assesses concepts students learned throughout the school year. The activities are similar to those in other assessment units. Students begin by reviewing past laboratory investigations. This prepares them for completing the experiment, *Area vs. Length,* which assesses their abilities to use and apply the TIMS Laboratory Method. An open-response problem, *The Many-Eyed Dragonfly,* is included to see if students can combine many of the skills they have acquired to solve a problem. Students then complete a short item test of concepts and skills taught in previous units. Finally, students review past work in their portfolios and compare it to recently completed work to see growth over time. The DPP includes a test on all the division facts.

Major Concept Focus

- TIMS Laboratory Method
- patterns in data
- number patterns
- point graphs
- area
- problem solving
- length
- portfolio review
- geometric patterns
- communicating problem-solving strategies
- end-of-year test
- division fact test
- Student Rubrics: *Solving, Knowing,* and *Telling*

Pacing Suggestions

This unit includes a variety of review and assessment activities that provide opportunities for teachers to assess individual growth in mathematics. Students continue learning as they apply concepts and skills in new contexts.

Lesson 2 *Problems and Practice* is an optional lesson. It is a set of problems that reviews skills and concepts and helps students prepare for the *End-of-Year Test* in Lesson 5. The problems can be assigned for homework.

Assessment Indicators

Use the following Assessment Indicators and the *Observational Assessment Record* that follows the Background section in this unit to assess students on key ideas.

A1. Can students identify and use variables?

A2. Can students collect, organize, graph, and analyze data?

A3. Can students use patterns in data to make predictions and solve problems?

A4. Can students solve open-response problems and communicate solution strategies?

A5. Do students demonstrate fluency with the division facts?

Unit Planner

(found in Discovery Assignment Book), and the Teacher Implementation Guide.

	Lesson Information	Supplies	Copies/ Transparencies
Lesson 1 **Experiment Review** URG Pages 23–39 SG Page 430 DAB Pages 251–252 DPP A–B HP Parts 1–2 *Estimated Class Sessions* **1**	**Activity** Students review the labs they worked on during the past year. They recount the various elements of each lab. **Math Facts** DPP Task B provides practice with division facts using the *Triangle Flash Cards*. **Homework** 1. The Journal Prompt may be assigned for homework. 2. Assign Part 2 of the Home Practice. 3. Lesson 2 of this unit, *Problems and Practice*, may be assigned as homework. **Assessment** Use the *Observational Assessment Record* to document students' understanding of the use of variables in experiments.	• 1 student portfolio per student	• 1 copy of *Triangle Flash Cards* URG Pages 32–38 per student, optional • 1 transparency of *Downhill Racer Graph* URG Page 31 • 1 copy of *Observational Assessment Record* URG Pages 9–10 to be used throughout this unit • 1 transparency of *Experiment Review Chart* DAB Pages 251–252 or large sheet of chart paper for class chart
Lesson 2 **Problems and Practice** URG Pages 40–45 SG Pages 431–434 *Estimated Class Sessions* **1**	OPTIONAL LESSON **Optional Activity** Students complete a series of applied problems. You can use these problems to review major concepts before the end-of-year test. **Homework** Assign the *Problems and Practice* Activity Pages.	• 1 calculator per student • pattern blocks • square-inch tiles • base-ten pieces, optional	
Lesson 3 **Area vs. Length** URG Pages 46–63 SG Pages 435–438 DPP C–H HP Parts 7–8 *Estimated Class Sessions* **3**	**Assessment Lab** Students use the TIMS Laboratory Method to investigate the relationship between area and length for rectangles of fixed width. **Math Facts** DPP Bit C provides practice with division facts. **Homework** Students complete Parts 7 and 8 of the Home Practice. **Assessment** 1. Use the *TIMS Multidimensional Rubric* or a point scale to assess students' abilities to implement the steps of the TIMS Laboratory Method. 2. Assess students' letters to Myrna using the Telling dimension of the *TIMS Multidimensional Rubric*. 3. Use the *Observational Assessment Record* to document students' abilities to collect, organize, graph, and analyze data.	• 50 square-inch tiles per student group • 1 ruler per student	• 1 copy of *Three-column Data Table* URG Page 59 per student • 1 copy of *Centimeter Graph Paper* URG Page 60 per student • 1 copy of *TIMS Multidimensional Rubric* TIG, Assessment section • 1 transparency or poster of Student Rubric: *Telling* TIG, Assessment section

	Lesson Information	Supplies	Copies/ Transparencies
Lesson 4 **The Many-Eyed Dragonfly** URG Pages 64–84 DPP I–L HP Parts 3–4 *Estimated Class Sessions* **2**	**Assessment Activity** Students identify and extend patterns to solve an open-response problem and write about their solutions. **Math Facts** DPP Bit I provides practice with math facts. **Homework** Assign Parts 3 and 4 of the Home Practice. **Assessment** Use the Solving, Knowing, and Telling dimensions of the *TIMS Multidimensional Rubric* to assess student work on *The Many-Eyed Dragonfly* Assessment Blackline Masters.	• square-inch tiles • 1 calculator per student	• 1 copy of *The Many-Eyed Dragonfly* URG Pages 77–80 per student • 1 copy of *Two-column Data Table* URG Page 81 per student • 1 transparency or poster of Student Rubrics: *Knowing, Solving,* and *Telling* TIG, Assessment section • 1 copy of *TIMS Multidimensional Rubric* TIG, Assessment section
Lesson 5 **End-of-Year Test** URG Pages 85–94 DPP M–P HP Parts 5–6 *Estimated Class Sessions* **2**	**Assessment Activity** Students complete a short item test on the concepts and skills taught in previous units. **Math Facts** DPP Bit O provides practice computing with multiples of 10 and Task P reviews multiplication and division with zeros and ones. **Homework** 1. Assign Parts 5 and 6 of the Home Practice either in this lesson or in Lesson 6. 2. Students study for the *Division Facts Inventory Test* using *Triangle Flash Cards.*	• 1 calculator per student • 1 ruler per student • pattern blocks • base-ten pieces	• 1 copy of *End-of-Year-Test* URG Pages 90–92 per student
Lesson 6 **Portfolios** URG Pages 95–99 SG Page 439 DPP Q–R *Estimated Class Sessions* **1-2**	**Assessment Activity** Students review the contents of their collection folders and their portfolio folders. Students select pieces to include in their final portfolios. **Math Facts** DPP Task R is an assessment of all the division facts. **Homework** Students share their portfolios with their parents for homework. **Assessment** 1. DPP Task R is the *Division Facts Inventory Test* and assesses fluency with the division facts. Record students' fluency with the division facts on the *Observational Assessment Record.* 2. Transfer appropriate Unit 16 observations to students' *Individual Assessment Record Sheets.*	• 1 portfolio folder from Unit 2 per student • 1 collection folder from Unit 2 per student • two different-colored pencils or a pen and pencil per student	• 1 copy of *Division Facts Inventory Test* URG Page 22 per student • 1 copy of *Individual Assessment Record Sheet* TIG Assessment section per student, previously copied for use throughout the year

Connections

A current list of literature and software connections is available at *www.mathtrailblazers.com.* You can also find information on connections in the *Teacher Implementation Guide* Literature List and Software List sections.

Software Connections

- *Graph Master* allows students to collect data and create their own graphs.
- *Kid Pix* allows students to create their own illustrations.
- *TinkerPlots* allows students to record, compare, and analyze data in tables and graphs.

Teaching All Math Trailblazers Students

Math Trailblazers® lessons are designed for students with a wide range of abilities. The lessons are flexible and do not require significant adaptation for diverse learning styles or academic levels. However, when needed, lessons can be tailored to allow students to engage their abilities to the greatest extent possible while building knowledge and skills.

To assist you in meeting the needs of all students in your classroom, this section contains information about some of the features in the curriculum that allow all students access to mathematics. For additional information, see the Teaching the *Math Trailblazers* Student: Meeting Individual Needs section in the *Teacher Implementation Guide.*

Differentiation Opportunities in this Unit

Laboratory Experiments

Laboratory experiments enable students to solve problems using a variety of representations including pictures, tables, graphs, and symbols. Teachers can assign or adapt parts of the analysis according to the student's ability. The following lesson is a lab:

- Lesson 3 *Area vs. Length*

Journal Prompts

Journal prompts provide opportunities for students to explain and reflect on mathematical problems. They can help both students who need practice explaining their ideas and students who benefit from answering higher order questions. Students with various learning styles can express themselves using pictures, words, and sentences. Teachers can alter journal prompts to suit students' ability levels. The following lessons contain a journal prompt:

- Lesson 1 *Experiment Review*
- Lesson 4 *The Many-Eyed Dragonfly*

DPP Challenges

DPP Challenges are items from the Daily Practice and Problems that usually take more than fifteen minutes to complete. These problems are more thought-provoking and can be used to stretch students' problem-solving skills. The following lessons have a DPP Challenge in them:

- DPP Challenge H from Lesson 3 *Area vs. Length*
- DPP Challenge J from Lesson 4 *The Many-Eyed Dragonfly*

Extensions

Use extensions to enrich lessons. Many extensions provide opportunities to further involve or challenge students of all abilities. Take a moment to review the extensions prior to beginning this unit. Some extensions may require additional preparation and planning. The following lesson contains an extension:

- Lesson 3 *Area vs. Length*

Unit 16

Background
Assessing Our Learning

This unit concludes the fourth-grade *Math Trailblazers* curriculum. The lessons review, extend, and assess concepts students learned throughout the school year. The activities are similar to those in other assessment units. This allows students to compare the work they complete in this unit with similar tasks in other units. For example, in the lab in Lesson 3 *Area vs. Length,* students find the relationship between the lengths and the areas of rectangles with fixed width. Students use data tables and graphs to identify patterns that help them find this relationship. This is similar to the work in the lab *Perimeter vs. Length* in Unit 2. When students compare their work on these labs, they look for their growth in mathematics.

During this unit, students will also complete the problem-solving task, *The Many-Eyed Dragonfly.* To solve this problem, students collect data, organize it in a table, and then look for patterns in the data. Finally, students communicate their problem-solving strategies. A short-item test covering content from the fourth-grade curriculum is provided in Lesson 5. In Lesson 6, the *Division Facts Inventory Test* appears as DPP Task R. As a final assessment activity, students review and add to their portfolios.

Students can compare their work on similar assessment activities completed in Units 2 and 8. Take

some time with your students to compare the work from these units. It is very beneficial for students to review their past work. Usually they can easily see their progress. These activities build students' mathematical confidence. The results of these assessment activities, combined with the information gathered through daily observations, provide a balanced assessment of each student's growth during the school year.

Resources

- *Assessment Standards for School Mathematics.* National Council of Teachers of Mathematics, Reston, VA, 1995.

- *Balanced Assessment for the Mathematics Curriculum Elementary Package.* Balanced Assessment Project, Berkeley, CA, 1995.

- National Research Council. *Knowing What Students Know: The Science and Design of Educational Assessment.* Committee on the Foundations of Assessment. J. Pelligrino, N. Chudowsky, and R. Glaser, eds. National Academy Press, Washington, DC, 2001.

- *Principles and Standards for School Mathematics.* National Council of Teachers of Mathematics, Reston, VA, March 2000.

Observational Assessment Record

(A1) Can students identify and use variables?

(A2) Can students collect, organize, graph, and analyze data?

(A3) Can students use patterns in data to make predictions and solve problems?

(A4) Can students solve open-response problems and communicate solution strategies?

(A5) Do students demonstrate fluency with the division facts?

(A6) _____

Name	A1	A2	A3	A4	A5	A6	Comments
1.							
2.							
3.							
4.							
5.							
6.							
7.							
8.							
9.							
10.							
11.							
12.							
13.							

Name	A1	A2	A3	A4	A5	A6	Comments
14.							
15.							
16.							
17.							
18.							
19.							
20.							
21.							
22.							
23.							
24.							
25.							
26.							
27.							
28.							
29.							
30.							
31.							
32.							

Unit 16

Daily Practice and Problems
Assessing Our Learning

A DPP Menu for Unit 16

Two Daily Practice and Problems (DPP) items are included for each class session listed in the Unit Outline. A scope and sequence chart for the DPP is in the *Teacher Implementation Guide*.

Icons in the Teacher Notes column designate the subject matter of each DPP item. The first item in each class session is always a Bit and the second is either a Task or Challenge. Each item falls into one or more of the categories listed below. A menu of the DPP items for Unit 16 follows.

N Number Sense	Computation	⏱ Time	Geometry
A, D, G, J–L, N–Q	A, H, K, L, O	M	E, F, N

5/x7 Math Facts	$ Money	Measurement	Data
B, C, I, O, P, R		E, F, J	

Practice and Assessment of the Division Facts

By the end of this unit, students are expected to demonstrate fluency with all the division facts. The DPP for this unit reviews the related division facts for all five groups of multiplication facts (2s and 3s, 5s and 10s, square numbers, 9s, and the last six facts—4×6, 4×7, 4×8, 6×7, 6×8, and 7×8). A test on the division facts is administered in DPP item R and is located at the end of the DPP section. Each group of facts flash cards are in Lesson 1 and in the *Grade 4 Facts Resource Guide*.

For more information about the distribution and assessment of the math facts, see the TIMS Tutor: *Math Facts* in the *Teacher Implementation Guide*. Also refer to the DPP guides in the *Unit Resource Guides* for Units 3 and 9.

Daily Practice and Problems

Students may solve the items individually, in groups, or as a class. The items may also be assigned for homework. The DPPs are also available on the Teacher Resource CD.

Student Questions	Teacher Notes

A **Addition and Subtraction**

1. Do the following problems in your head.

   A. $45 + 25 =$

   B. $88 + 102 =$

   C. $109 - 11 =$

   D. $872 - 865 =$

   E. $197 + 5 =$

   F. $2003 - 500 =$

2. Explain your mental math strategy for Questions C and F.

TIMS Bit

Encourage students to share strategies.

1. A. 70
   B. 190
   C. 98
   D. 7
   E. 202
   F. 1503

2. Answers will vary. A possible strategy for C: 11 is 2 more than 9, $109 - 9 = 100$, minus 2 more $= 98$. A possible strategy for F: $2000 - 500$ is 1500 and 3 more is 1503.

B Division Facts

With a partner, use your *Triangle Flash Cards* to quiz each other on all the division facts. One partner uses his or her thumb to cover the corner containing the number in a square. The second person solves a division fact using the two uncovered numbers. Go through the cards a second time, this time covering the corner containing the number in a circle.

After each time through the cards, separate them into three piles: those facts you know and can answer quickly, those you can figure out with a strategy, and those you need to study. Practice the last two piles again and then list the facts you need to practice at home for homework.

Circle the facts you know and can answer quickly on your *Division Facts I Know* chart.

TIMS Task

Students used the flash cards to review all five groups of facts in Units 14 and 15. For those students who need new copies, masters for the flash cards can be found in Lesson 1. After students sort the cards, they should continue to practice the facts in the last two piles—those facts they can figure out with a strategy and those they need to learn. Discuss strategies students use to find the answers to the facts, emphasizing the more efficient strategies.

Encourage students to list the facts they need to practice at home for homework as well as update their *Division Facts I Know* chart. In Part 1 of the Home Practice, students are reminded to bring home their *Triangle Flash Cards* for the division facts.

An inventory test on all the facts is given in DPP item R. Inform students when you will give the test.

C Division Facts Practice

1. A. $50 \div 5 =$ B. $12 \div 3 =$

   C. $90 \div 10 =$ D. $0 \div 8 =$

   E. $24 \div 8 =$ F. $28 \div 7 =$

   G. $56 \div 8 =$ H. $80 \div 8 =$

   I. $4 \div 4 =$ J. $48 \div 8 =$

2. Explain your strategy for Question 1G.

TIMS Bit

1. A. 10
   B. 4
   C. 9
   D. 0
   E. 3
   F. 4
   G. 7
   H. 10
   I. 1
   J. 6
2. Strategies will vary.

D Rounding Numbers

1. Order the numbers below from smallest to largest.

   A. 780,188   B. 708,589

   C. 89,524   D. 190,776

   E. 17,460   F. 4,239,454

2. Find at least two ways to round each of the numbers above.

TIMS Task

1. 17,460; 89,524; 190,776; 708,589; 780,188; 4,239,454

2. Answers will vary. Two possible answers are given for each.
   A. 800,000 and 780,000
   B. 700,000 and 709,000
   C. 90,000 and 89,500
   D. 191,000 and 200,000
   E. 20,000 and 17,000
   F. 4,000,000 and 4,200,000

E **Area and Perimeter**

1. What is the area of the rectangle below?

2 inches

3 inches

2. What is the perimeter?

TIMS Bit

Use this bit as an introduction to Lesson 3 *Area vs. Length*. Review area and perimeter and the units of measure for each.

1. 6 square inches

2. 10 inches

F **More Area and Perimeter**

A rectangle is 4 cm wide. Its length is twice as long as its width.

1. Draw this rectangle. You may use a piece of *Centimeter Grid Paper.*

2. What is the area of the rectangle?

3. What is the perimeter of the rectangle?

TIMS Task

1. 4 cm

8 cm

2. 32 sq cm

3. 24 cm

Student Questions	Teacher Notes

G **Fractions**

Which is larger:

A. $\frac{1}{12}$ or $\frac{1}{10}$?

B. $\frac{3}{2}$ or $1\frac{1}{4}$?

C. $\frac{6}{12}$ or 0.5?

D. $\frac{5}{8}$ or 0.4?

Be prepared to explain how you decided on your answers.

TIMS Bit [N]

Discuss student strategies.

A. $\frac{1}{10}$

B. $\frac{3}{2}$

C. They are equal.

D. $\frac{5}{8}$

H **Solving Problems**

1. A tailor spent half his money on cotton cloth and half on wool cloth. He bought 10 yards of cotton and 2 yards of wool. The cotton cost $2 per yard. How much was the wool per yard?

2. An art teacher has to order construction paper for next year. She ordered 300 packages of construction paper. Each of the 15 primary-grade classes needs 12 packages of paper for the entire school year. The rest of the paper is evenly shared among the 10 intermediate-grade classes. How many packages do each of the intermediate classes receive?

TIMS Challenge ▨

1. The cotton cost $2 × 10 = $20.

   He spent $20 on wool as well so the wool must have cost $10 per yard.

2. The primary grades will receive 12 × 15 or 180 packages. This leaves 120 packages to be shared among the intermediate grades. Each class will receive 12 packages.

Student Questions	Teacher Notes

I **Fact Families for × and ÷**

Solve each fact. Then name the three other facts in the same fact family. The square numbers have only two facts in each family.

A. $8 \times 3 =$

B. $30 \div 6 =$

C. $64 \div 8 =$

D. $9 \times 7 =$

E. $24 \div 4 =$

F. $6 \times 6 =$

G. $36 \div 4 =$

H. $8 \times 4 =$

I. $42 \div 7 =$

J. $6 \times 9 =$

TIMS Bit $\boxed{\times\frac{5}{7}}$

Complete this item orally as a class. One student can solve the given fact and other students can name each of the other related facts.

A. 24; $3 \times 8 = 24$;
   $24 \div 3 = 8$; $24 \div 8 = 3$

B. 5; $30 \div 5 = 6$;
   $5 \times 6 = 30$; $6 \times 5 = 30$

C. 8; $8 \times 8 = 64$

D. 63; $7 \times 9 = 63$;
   $63 \div 7 = 9$; $63 \div 9 = 7$

E. 6; $24 \div 6 = 4$;
   $6 \times 4 = 24$; $4 \times 6 = 24$

F. 36; $36 \div 6 = 6$

G. 9; $36 \div 9 = 4$;
   $4 \times 9 = 36$; $9 \times 4 = 36$

H. 32; $4 \times 8 = 32$;
   $32 \div 4 = 8$; $32 \div 8 = 4$

I. 6; $42 \div 6 = 7$;
   $6 \times 7 = 42$; $7 \times 6 = 42$

J. 54; $9 \times 6 = 54$;
   $54 \div 9 = 6$; $54 \div 6 = 9$

J **Measurement**

1. Write the measurements below in order from shortest to longest.

   A. 5 cm   B. 60 cm

   C. 4 dm   D. 1 m 14 cm

   E. 125 cm

2. Write each measurement in meters.

TIMS Challenge 🎢 Ⓝ

1. 5 cm, 4 dm, 60 cm, 1 m 14 cm, 125 cm

2. 0.05 m, 0.6 m, 0.4 m, 1.14 m, 1.25 m

Student Questions	Teacher Notes

K **More Addition and Subtraction**

1. Use paper and pencil or mental math to solve the following problems. Estimate to be sure your answers are reasonable.

   A. $7909 + 257 =$

   B. $7854 - 75 =$

   C. $2317 + 905 =$

   D. $2065 - 978 =$

2. Explain a mental math strategy for Question 1C.

TIMS Bit ⊠ N

1. A. 8166

   B. 7779

   C. 3222

   D. 1087

2. One possible strategy:
   $2300 + 900 = 3200$;
   $17 + 5 = 22$;
   $3200 + 22 = 3222$.

L **Multiplication and Division**

Solve the following problems using paper and pencil or mental math. Estimate to be sure your answers are reasonable.

1. A. $56 \times 70 =$ B. $68 \times 19 =$

   C. $293 \times 4 =$ D. $354 \div 6 =$

   E. $2618 \div 9 =$ F. $3012 \div 4 =$

2. Explain your estimation strategy for Question 1B.

TIMS Task ⊠ N

1. A. 3920

   B. 1292

   C. 1172

   D. 59

   E. 290 R8

   F. 753

2. One possible strategy:
   Round 68×19 to 70×20;
   $7 \times 2 = 14$;
   $70 \times 20 = 1400$.

(M) Time

1. John ate dinner 2 hours and 15 minutes after he got home from school. If he ate dinner at 5:20, what time did he get home from school?

2. Shannon took her little cousin to the park. They left the house at 4:15. It took them 20 minutes to walk to the park. They played for 45 minutes and then walked back home. What time did they arrive home?

TIMS Bit 🕐

1. 3:05
2. 5:40

(N) Pattern Block Fractions

If the shape below is one whole, name the fraction each shape in A–D represents.

A.

B.

C.

D.

TIMS Task N 🖾

If needed, encourage students to use pattern blocks.

A. $\frac{1}{8}$

B. $\frac{3}{8}$

C. $\frac{2}{8}$ or $\frac{1}{4}$

D. $\frac{4}{8}$ or $\frac{1}{2}$

Student Questions	Teacher Notes

◉ Multiplying with Zeros

The *n* in each number sentence stands for a missing number. Find the number that makes each sentence true.

A. $80 \times n = 320$

B. $n \times 30 = 27{,}000$

C. $8000 \times n = 56{,}000$

D. $50 \times n = 10{,}000$

E. $400 \times n = 40{,}000$

F. $300 \times n = 1500$

Ⓟ Zeros and Ones

1. A. $8 \times 1 =$ B. $4 \div 0 =$

   C. $0 \div 9 =$ D. $1 \div 1 =$

   E. $12 \div 1 =$ F. $5 \div 0 =$

   G. $7 \times 0 =$ H. $3 \div 3 =$

2. Justify your reasoning for Questions 1B and 1C using a related multiplication sentence.

Ⓠ United States Population

In 1790 the first U.S. census was taken. There were 3,929,200 people in the United States. By 2000 there were 281,421,906 people in the United States.

1. About how many more people were there in 2000 as compared to 1790?

2. This change in population occurred over how many years?

| | | Student Questions | | | Teacher Notes | |

R Division Facts Inventory Test

Have two pens or pencils of different colors ready. During the first four minutes of the test, write the answers using one color pen or pencil. After four minutes, complete the remaining items with the other color pen or pencil.

TIMS Task

Students take the *Division Facts Inventory Test*. We recommend four minutes for this test. After four minutes, allow students to change to different colored pencils or pens and complete the test.

Since students learned the division facts through their work with fact families, if a student knows $27 \div 3 = 9$, he or she most likely knows that $27 \div 9 = 3$. To make sure, after the test ask students to write a related division fact for each fact on the test (other than the facts for the square numbers). Students then update their *Division Facts I Know* charts for the last time and place both this test and the chart in their portfolios.

1. 2	2. 8	3. 2	4. 8
5. 8	6. 5	7. 4	8. 3
9. 3	10. 3	11. 3	12. 10
13. 3	14. 7	15. 9	16. 6
17. 8	18. 7	19. 9	20. 5
21. 10	22. 4	23. 9	24. 2
25. 2	26. 8	27. 2	28. 10
29. 5	30. 0	31. 8	32. 6
33. 4	34. 9	35. 6	36. 5
37. 8	38. 10	39. 7	40. 3
41. 5	42. 6	43. 1	44. 3
45. 5	46. 5	47. 10	48. 6

Division Facts Inventory Test

1. $18 \div 9 =$ 2. $40 \div 5 =$ 3. $4 \div 2 =$ 4. $80 \div 10 =$

5. $72 \div 9 =$ 6. $30 \div 6 =$ 7. $12 \div 3 =$ 8. $21 \div 7 =$

9. $6 \div 2 =$ 10. $18 \div 6 =$ 11. $27 \div 9 =$ 12. $40 \div 4 =$

13. $9 \div 3 =$ 14. $35 \div 5 =$ 15. $63 \div 7 =$ 16. $48 \div 8 =$

17. $32 \div 4 =$ 18. $42 \div 6 =$ 19. $36 \div 4 =$ 20. $5 \div 1 =$

21. $90 \div 9 =$ 22. $16 \div 4 =$ 23. $81 \div 9 =$ 24. $16 \div 8 =$

25. $8 \div 4 =$ 26. $24 \div 3 =$ 27. $14 \div 7 =$ 28. $100 \div 10 =$

29. $10 \div 2 =$ 30. $0 \div 9 =$ 31. $64 \div 8 =$ 32. $60 \div 10 =$

33. $28 \div 7 =$ 34. $54 \div 6 =$ 35. $36 \div 6 =$ 36. $45 \div 9 =$

37. $56 \div 7 =$ 38. $20 \div 2 =$ 39. $49 \div 7 =$ 40. $30 \div 10 =$

41. $25 \div 5 =$ 42. $24 \div 4 =$ 43. $7 \div 7 =$ 44. $15 \div 5 =$

45. $20 \div 4 =$ 46. $50 \div 10 =$ 47. $70 \div 7 =$ 48. $12 \div 2 =$

Experiment Review

Lesson Overview

Estimated Class Sessions

1

Students review the labs they worked on during the second half of the year by recounting elements of each lab: variables, number of trials, type of graph, problems solved, and so on. They will use their work, the *Student Guide,* and their portfolios to help them recall each lab. The class discusses the similarities and differences of the experiments.

Key Content

- Comparing and contrasting the following elements of different experiments:

  variables

  measurement procedures

  number of trials

  types of graphs

  problems solved
- Reflecting on past work.

Key Vocabulary

- bar graph
- best-fit line
- point graph
- trial
- variable

Math Facts

DPP Task B provides practice with the division facts using the *Triangle Flash Cards.*

Homework

1. The Journal Prompt may be assigned for homework.
2. Assign Part 2 of the Home Practice.
3. Lesson 2 of this unit, *Problems and Practice,* may be assigned as homework.

Assessment

Use the *Observational Assessment Record* to document students' understanding of the use of variables in experiments.

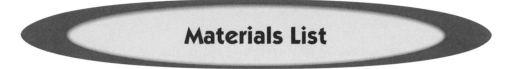

Curriculum Sequence

Before This Unit

Review Chart

In Unit 8 Lesson 7, students completed a similar chart for the labs completed in Units 1–8.

Materials List

Supplies and Copies

Student	Teacher
Supplies for Each Student • student portfolio	**Supplies**
Copies • 1 copy of *Triangle Flash Cards* per student, optional (*Unit Resource Guide* Pages 32–38)	**Copies/Transparencies** • 1 transparency of *Downhill Racer Graph* (*Unit Resource Guide* Page 31) • 1 copy of *Observational Assessment Record* to be used throughout this unit (*Unit Resource Guide* Pages 9–10) • 1 transparency of *Experiment Review Chart* or large sheet of chart paper for class chart (*Discovery Assignment Book* Pages 251–252)

All blackline masters including assessment, transparency, and DPP masters are also on the Teacher Resource CD.

Student Books
Experiment Review (*Student Guide* Page 430)
Experiment Review Chart (*Discovery Assignment Book* Pages 251–252)

Daily Practice and Problems and Home Practice
DPP items A–B (*Unit Resource Guide* Pages 12–13)
Home Practice Parts 1–2 (*Discovery Assignment Book* Page 247)

Note: Classrooms whose pacing differs significantly from the suggested pacing of the units should use the Math Facts Calendar in Section 4 of the *Facts Resource Guide* to ensure students receive the complete math facts program.

Assessment Tools
Observational Assessment Record (*Unit Resource Guide* Pages 9–10)

Daily Practice and Problems

Suggestions for using the DPPs are on page 29.

A. Bit: Addition and Subtraction ※ N
(URG p. 12)

1. Do the following problems in your head.
   A. $45 + 25 =$
   B. $88 + 102 =$
   C. $109 - 11 =$
   D. $872 - 865 =$
   E. $197 + 5 =$
   F. $2003 - 500 =$
2. Explain your mental math strategy for Questions C and F.

B. Task: Division Facts (URG p. 13) $\frac{5}{\times 7}$

With a partner, use your *Triangle Flash Cards* to quiz each other on all the division facts. One partner uses his or her thumb to cover the corner containing the number in a square. The second person solves a division fact using the two uncovered numbers. Go through the cards a second time, this time covering the corner containing the number in a circle.

After each time through the cards, separate them into three piles: those facts you know and can answer quickly, those you can figure out with a strategy, and those you need to study. Practice the last two piles again and then list the facts you need to practice at home for homework.

Circle the facts you know and can answer quickly on your *Division Facts I Know* chart.

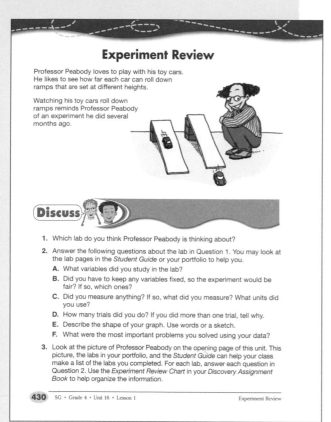

Experiment Review

Professor Peabody loves to play with his toy cars. He likes to see how far each car can roll down ramps that are set at different heights.

Watching his toy cars roll down ramps reminds Professor Peabody of an experiment he did several months ago.

Discuss

1. Which lab do you think Professor Peabody is thinking about?

2. Answer the following questions about the lab in Question 1. You may look at the lab pages in the *Student Guide* or your portfolio to help you.
   A. What variables did you study in the lab?
   B. Did you have to keep any variables fixed, so the experiment would be fair? If so, which ones?
   C. Did you measure anything? If so, what did you measure? What units did you use?
   D. How many trials did you do? If you did more than one trial, tell why.
   E. Describe the shape of your graph. Use words or a sketch.
   F. What were the most important problems you solved using your data?

3. Look at the picture of Professor Peabody on the opening page of this unit. This picture, the labs in your portfolio, and the *Student Guide* can help your class make a list of the labs you completed. For each lab, answer each question in Question 2. Use the *Experiment Review Chart* in your *Discovery Assignment Book* to help organize the information.

430 SG • Grade 4 • Unit 16 • Lesson 1   Experiment Review

Student Guide - page 430 *(Answers on p. 39)*

Begin this activity by reading the vignette on the *Experiment Review* Activity Page in the *Student Guide*. As he rolls cars down ramps, Professor Peabody remembers the lab *Downhill Racer* from Unit 10. This sets a context for a class discussion reviewing the various labs completed this year.

Begin your review by discussing the lab *Downhill Racer,* using **Question 2** as a guide. Have students use the *Experiment Review Chart* Activity Pages in the *Discovery Assignment Book* to organize their information. Students begin by writing *Downhill Racer* at the top of the second column. They then fill in that column with information about the lab. See Figure 1. A transparency master of one *Downhill Racer Graph* is included in the Lesson Guide to help students answer the questions about this lab. Note that **Question 2E** in the *Student Guide* asks students to describe the shape of the graph. Encourage students to draw a sketch of the graph.

TIMS Tip

If students did not complete the lab *Downhill Racer,* use a different lab to launch this discussion.

Name _____ Date _____

Experiment Review Chart

Directions:
- Write the names of the experiments completed this year in the first row of the table.
- Complete each column with information from each lab.

Name of Experiment → / Experiment Elements ↓			
Main Variables			
Fixed Variables			
Anything Measured (units)			
Number of Trials			
Type of Graph			
Important Questions (Answers may vary.)			

Experiment Review   DAB • Grade 4 • Unit 16 • Lesson 1 **251**

Discovery Assignment Book - page 251

After the class discussion of *Downhill Racer,* **Question 3** asks students to recall other labs they completed this year and to make a list of them. Students can look through their *Student Guides* or portfolios to help them recall the different labs. In the *Student Guide,* the picture facing the Table of Contents for this unit provides clues or reminders of the labs completed in the second half of the year. Note that the activity, *TV Survey* from Unit 13, is included in the chart since it includes many elements of a lab. Once this list is complete, divide the class into groups of two to four students. Assign each group one or two labs on the list and ask them to review the lab using **Question 2** and the *Experiment Review Chart* as guides.

Once all the groups complete their reviews, each group shares their information with the class. Organize the information on a class chart using large chart paper or on transparencies of the *Experiment Review Chart* as shown in Figure 1. Answers shown in this chart are sample answers. Your class responses may vary from the responses shown here. Once the class chart is complete, each student records the information on his or her individual *Experiment Review Chart.*

If you wish to include laboratory investigations from Units 1–8, see Lesson Guide 7 in Unit 8.

After compiling the class information, continue the discussion by comparing and contrasting the various labs. Some possible discussion questions follow:

- *When doing an experiment, why do you need to keep some variables fixed?* (To be able to look for patterns and make predictions using the main variables in an experiment, other variables must be held fixed. Students often think of holding variables fixed in an experiment as "keeping the experiment fair." For example, in the experiment *Downhill Racer,* to make predictions about how far the car will roll when released on a ramp of a certain height, you must use the same car and release it from the same starting point.)

- *Why do we often have to do more than one trial when doing an experiment?* (One reason scientists use multiple trials is to check on errors in measurement and in controlling fixed variables.

Discovery Assignment Book - page 252

TIMS Tip

If students did not complete all the labs during the school year, adjust the chart as needed.

Experiment Elements	Downhill Racer	Rolling One Number Cube	TV Survey	Plant Growth	Taste of TIMS
Main Variables	height of ramp, distance the car travels	faces on the cube, number of times each face is rolled	hours of TV watched, number of students	time, height of plant	number of bites, mass of sandwich
Fixed Variables	car type, floor surface, method of launching car, procedure to measure ramp height and distance		collect data on same 4 days, record only your TV time, record time before and after school, define TV time, how time is recorded	amount of sunlight, type of soil, volume of soil, number of seeds, type of seed, volume of water	bite size
Anything Measured (units)	ramp height (cm), distance the car travels (m)	No	time (minutes/hours)	plant height (cm), time (days)	mass of sandwich (grams)
Number of Trials	3	N/A	N/A	1	1
Type of Graph					
Important Questions (Answers may vary.)	Given the height of the ramp, predict the distance the car will roll.	What is the probability that you will roll a given number using one number cube?	On average, how many hours do fourth-grade students watch TV daily?	What are the growth patterns of plants?	What is the mass of a student's average-size bite? Predict the number of bites to eat the entire sandwich.

Figure 1: *Sample* Experiment Review *class chart of second semester labs*

Error is often inevitable, so scientists use multiple trials so they can average out the error. However, if large errors in measurement are not likely, one trial may suffice. Students may discuss the multiple trials that they took in *Bouncing Ball* and *Downhill Racer.* In both these labs, students took multiple trials and then used either the mean or the median to average out error.)

- *How are point graphs used to make predictions?* (If the points suggest a straight line, a line can be drawn to fit the points. This line is called the best-fit line. You can use this line to interpolate and extrapolate information. Students can discuss the different point graphs they made in fourth grade. They may talk about the differences between the point graphs in *Perimeter vs. Length, Bouncing Ball, Downhill Racer,* and *Taste of TIMS.* In *Perimeter vs. Length* and *Taste of TIMS,* the best-fit lines do not go through the data point (0,0), while in *Bouncing Ball* and *Downhill Racer,* the lines do go through (0,0). Students may also point out that the best-fit line drawn on the *Taste of TIMS* graph has a line that goes downhill when looking at the graph from left to right.)

Journal Prompt

Which two experiments did you like best? What did you like about each one? How are they alike? How are they different?

Math Facts

- DPP Task B is practice of the division facts using the *Triangle Flash Cards*.
- Home Practice Part 1 in the *Discovery Assignment Book* reminds students to take home their *Triangle Flash Cards* to study for the *Division Facts Inventory Test*. Encourage students to concentrate on those facts not yet circled on their *Division Facts I Know* charts.

Homework and Practice

- Assign the problems in Lesson 2 *Problems and Practice* as homework to review for the *End-of-Year Test* in Lesson 5.
- Assign the Journal Prompt as homework.
- DPP Bit A provides practice in mental addition and subtraction.
- Assign Part 2 of the Home Practice in the *Discovery Assignment Book*.

Answers for Part 2 of the Home Practice are in the Answer Key at the end of this lesson and at the end of this unit.

Assessment

The class discussions can provide an indication of whether students can identify and use variables. Record your observations on the *Observational Assessment Record*.

Name _____ Date _____

Unit 16 Home Practice

PART 1 *Triangle Flash Cards: All the Facts*
Study for the test on all the division facts. Take home your *Triangle Flash Cards* and your list of facts you need to study.

Here's how to use the flash cards. Ask a family member to choose one flash card at a time. He or she should cover the corner containing the number in a square. This number will be the answer to a division fact. Solve a division fact with the two uncovered numbers. Go through the cards a second time, this time covering the numbers in the circles.

Your teacher will tell you when the test on all the facts will be. Remember to concentrate on those facts you cannot answer correctly and quickly.

PART 2 Multiplication Tables
Complete the following tables.

1.

×	7	4	6	2	9
8					
3	12				
5					
1					

2.

×	10	5	6	3	0
8					
4	20				
2					
1					

3. Complete the following. Remember to follow the correct order of operations. Do all multiplications before any addition and subtraction. For example,
$4 + 100 \times 3 =$
$4 + 300 = 304.$

A. $7 \times 100 + 3 =$ _____ B. $6 + 800 \times 7 =$ _____

C. $5000 - 400 \times 5 =$ _____ D. $20 \times 20 + 350 =$ _____

E. $600 \times 80 - 2000 =$ _____ F. $20,000 - 18,000 \times 1 =$ _____

ASSESSING OUR LEARNING   DAB • Grade 4 • Unit 16 **247**

Copyright © Kendall/Hunt Publishing Company

Discovery Assignment Book - page 247 *(Answers on p. 39)*

URG • Grade 4 • Unit 16 • Lesson 1   **29**

Estimated Class Sessions

1

At a Glance

Math Facts and Daily Practice and Problems

DPP Bit A involves mental math practice. Task B provides practice with the division facts using the *Triangle Flash Cards*.

Teaching the Activity

1. Read the opening paragraph on the *Experiment Review* Activity Page in the *Student Guide*.
2. Review the lab *Downhill Racer* using **Question 2** in the *Student Guide,* a transparency of *Downhill Racer Graph*, and the *Experiment Review Chart* in the *Discovery Assignment Book*.
3. Use this unit's opening picture and **Question 3** in the *Student Guide* to help students recall the experiments they have done this year. Make a list of these labs.
4. Students work in groups to review labs completed throughout the year using their portfolios, *Experiment Review Chart,* and **Question 2** in the *Student Guide*.
5. Compile the class data on one class table. Students record the data on their own *Experiment Review Charts.*
6. Students compare and contrast labs to find similarities and differences.

Homework

1. The Journal Prompt may be assigned for homework.
2. Assign Part 2 of the Home Practice.
3. Lesson 2 of this unit, *Problems and Practice,* may be assigned as homework.

Assessment

Use the *Observational Assessment Record* to document students' understanding of the use of variables in experiments.

Answer Key is on page 39.

Notes:

Downhill Racer Graph

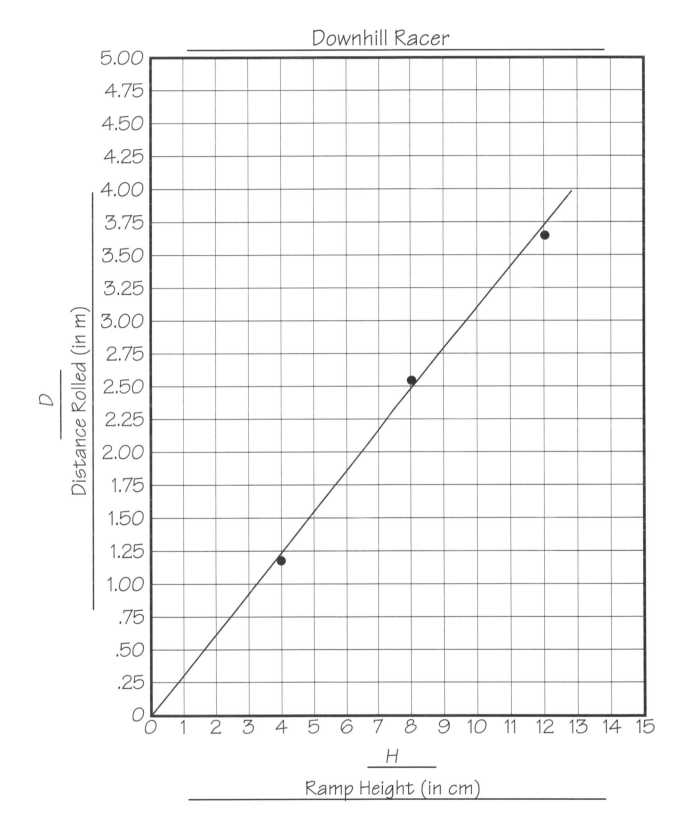

Downhill Racer

Distance Rolled (in m) $\dfrac{D}{}$

Ramp Height (in cm) $\dfrac{H}{}$

Triangle Flash Cards: 2s

- Work with a partner. Each partner cuts out the 9 flash cards.
- Your partner chooses one card at a time and covers one corner.
- To quiz you on a multiplication fact, your partner covers the shaded number. Multiply the two uncovered numbers.
- To quiz you on a division fact, your partner covers the number in the square or the number in the circle. Solve a division fact with the two uncovered numbers.
- Divide the used cards into three piles: those you know and can answer quickly, those you can figure out, and those you need to learn.
- Practice the last two piles again. Then make a list of the facts you need to practice at home.
- Repeat the directions for your partner.

Blackline Master

Triangle Flash Cards: 3s

- Work with a partner. Each partner cuts out the 9 flash cards.
- Your partner chooses one card at a time and covers one corner.
- To quiz you on a multiplication fact, your partner covers the shaded number. Multiply the two uncovered numbers.
- To quiz you on a division fact, your partner covers the number in the square or the number in the circle. Solve a division fact with the two uncovered numbers.
- Divide the used cards into three piles: those you know and can answer quickly, those you can figure out, and those you need to learn.
- Practice the last two piles again. Then make a list of the facts you need to practice at home.
- Repeat the directions for your partner.

Triangle Flash Cards: 5s

- Work with a partner. Each partner cuts out the 9 flash cards.
- Your partner chooses one card at a time and covers one corner.
- To quiz you on a multiplication fact, your partner covers the shaded number. Multiply the two uncovered numbers.
- To quiz you on a division fact, your partner covers the number in the square or the number in the circle. Solve a division fact with the two uncovered numbers.
- Divide the used cards into three piles: those you know and can answer quickly, those you can figure out, and those you need to learn.
- Practice the last two piles again. Then make a list of the facts you need to practice at home.
- Repeat the directions for your partner.

Copyright © Kendall/Hunt Publishing Company

Blackline Master

Triangle Flash Cards: 9s

- Work with a partner. Each partner cuts out the 9 flash cards.
- Your partner chooses one card at a time and covers one corner.
- To quiz you on a multiplication fact, your partner covers the shaded number. Multiply the two uncovered numbers.
- To quiz you on a division fact, your partner covers the number in the square or the number in the circle. Solve a division fact with the two uncovered numbers.
- Divide the used cards into three piles: those you know and can answer quickly, those you can figure out, and those you need to learn.
- Practice the last two piles again. Then make a list of the facts you need to practice at home.
- Repeat the directions for your partner.

Triangle Flash Cards: 10s

- Work with a partner. Each partner cuts out the 9 flash cards.
- Your partner chooses one card at a time and covers one corner.
- To quiz you on a multiplication fact, your partner covers the shaded number. Multiply the two uncovered numbers.
- To quiz you on a division fact, your partner covers the number in the square or the number in the circle. Solve a division fact with the two uncovered numbers.
- Divide the used cards into three piles: those you know and can answer quickly, those you can figure out, and those you need to learn.
- Practice the last two piles again. Then make a list of the facts you need to practice at home.
- Repeat the directions for your partner.

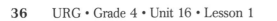

Triangle Flash Cards: Square Numbers

- Work with a partner. Each partner cuts out the 9 flash cards.
- Your partner chooses one card at a time and covers one corner.
- To quiz you on a multiplication fact, your partner covers the shaded number. Multiply the two uncovered numbers.
- To quiz you on a division fact, your partner covers one of the smaller numbers on each card. Solve a division fact with the two uncovered numbers.
- Divide the used cards into three piles: those you know and can answer quickly, those you can figure out, and those you need to learn.
- Practice the last two piles again. Then make a list of the facts you need to practice at home.
- Repeat the directions for your partner.

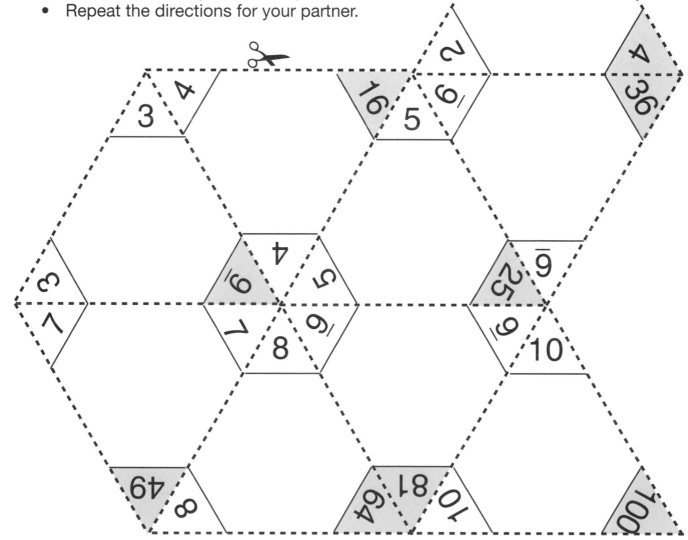

Triangle Flash Cards: The Last Six Facts

- Work with a partner. Each partner cuts out the 6 flash cards.
- Your partner chooses one card at a time and covers one corner.
- To quiz you on a multiplication fact, your partner covers the shaded number. Multiply the two uncovered numbers.
- To quiz you on a division fact, your partner covers the number in the square or the number in the circle. Solve a division fact with the two uncovered numbers.
- Divide the used cards into three piles: those you know and can answer quickly, those you can figure out, and those you need to learn.
- Practice the last two piles again. Then make a list of the facts you need to practice at home.
- Repeat the directions for your partner.

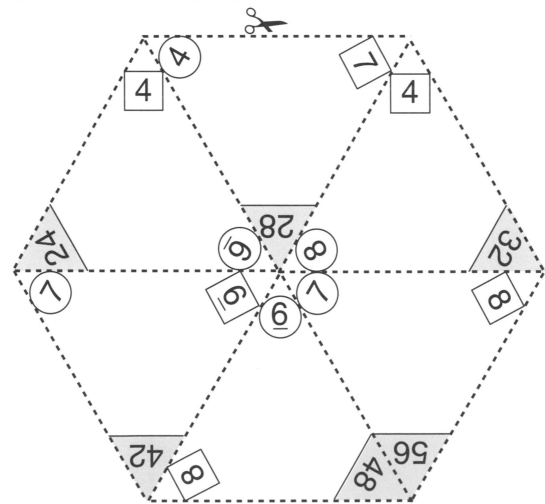

Student Guide (p. 430)

Experiment Review

1. Downhill Racer*

2.* A. height of ramp (H) and distance (D) the car travels

   B. type of car, floor surface, method of release, procedure to measure ramp height and distance car rolled

   C. ramp height in cm and distance the car travels in m

   D. 3 trials, to average out the error

   E. The graph is a straight line that slants uphill from the point ($H = 0$ cm, $D = 0$ m).

   F. Predicting the distance the car rolled for a given height. (Answers may vary.)

3. See Figure 1 in Lesson Guide 1.*

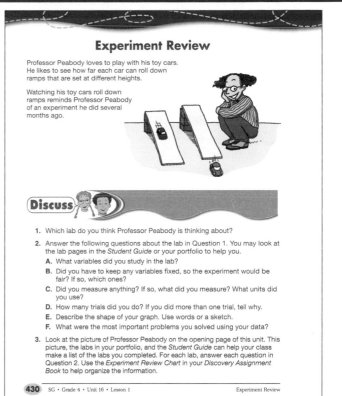

Experiment Review

Professor Peabody loves to play with his toy cars. He likes to see how far each car can roll down ramps that are set at different heights.

Watching his toy cars roll down ramps reminds Professor Peabody of an experiment he did several months ago.

Discuss

1. Which lab do you think Professor Peabody is thinking about?

2. Answer the following questions about the lab in Question 1. You may look at the lab pages in the *Student Guide* or your portfolio to help you.
   A. What variables did you study in the lab?
   B. Did you have to keep any variables fixed, so the experiment would be fair? If so, which ones?
   C. Did you measure anything? If so, what did you measure? What units did you use?
   D. How many trials did you do? If you did more than one trial, tell why.
   E. Describe the shape of your graph. Use words or a sketch.
   F. What were the most important problems you solved using your data?

3. Look at the picture of Professor Peabody on the opening page of this unit. This picture, the labs in your portfolio, and the *Student Guide* can help your class make a list of the labs you completed. For each lab, answer each question in Question 2. Use the *Experiment Review Chart* in your *Discovery Assignment Book* to help organize the information.

430 SG • Grade 4 • Unit 16 • Lesson 1   Experiment Review

Student Guide - page 430

Discovery Assignment Book (p. 247)

Home Practice†

Part 2. Multiplication Tables

1.

×	7	4	6	2	9
8	56	32	48	16	72
3	21	12	18	6	27
5	35	20	30	10	45
1	7	4	6	2	9

2.

×	10	5	6	3	0
8	80	40	48	24	0
4	40	20	24	12	0
2	20	10	12	6	0
1	10	5	6	3	0

3. A. 703   B. 5606

   C. 3000   D. 750

   E. 46,000   F. 2000

Name _____ Date _____

Unit 16 Home Practice

PART 1 *Triangle Flash Cards: All the Facts*

Study for the test on all the division facts. Take home your *Triangle Flash Cards* and your list of facts you need to study.

Here's how to use the flash cards. Ask a family member to choose one flash card at a time. He or she should cover the corner containing the number in a square. This number will be the answer to a division fact. Solve a division fact with the two uncovered numbers. Go through the cards a second time, this time covering the numbers in the circles.

Your teacher will tell you when the test on all the facts will be. Remember to concentrate on those facts you cannot answer correctly and quickly.

PART 2 **Multiplication Tables**
Complete the following tables.

1.

×	7	4	6	2	9
8					
3	12				
5					
1					

2.

×	10	5	6	3	0
8					
4	20				
2					
1					

3. Complete the following. Remember to follow the correct order of operations. Do all multiplications before any addition and subtraction. For example,
   $4 + 100 \times 3 =$
   $4 + 300 = 304$.

   A. $7 \times 100 + 3 =$ _____
   B. $6 + 800 \times 7 =$ _____
   C. $5000 - 400 \times 5 =$ _____
   D. $20 \times 20 + 350 =$ _____
   E. $600 \times 80 - 2000 =$ _____
   F. $20,000 - 18,000 \times 1 =$ _____

ASSESSING OUR LEARNING   DAB • Grade 4 • Unit 16 **247**

Discovery Assignment Book - page 247

*Answers and/or discussion are included in the Lesson Guide.
†Answers for all the Home Practice in the *Discovery Assignment Book* are at the end of the unit.

Optional Lesson 2

Problems and Practice

Lesson Overview

Estimated Class Sessions

1

Students complete a series of applied problems. These problems review major concepts taught in fourth grade. This lesson can serve as a review before the *End-of-Year Test* (Lesson 5) or as homework after the *Experiment Review* (Lesson 1).

Key Content

- Reviewing concepts and skills from previous units.
- Choosing appropriate methods and tools to solve problems.
- Choosing whether to find an estimate or an exact answer.

Homework

Assign the *Problems and Practice* Activity Pages.

Materials List

Supplies and Copies

Student	Teacher
Supplies for Each Student • calculator • pattern blocks • square-inch tiles • base-ten pieces, optional	**Supplies**
Copies	**Copies/Transparencies**

All blackline masters including assessment, transparency, and DPP masters are also on the Teacher Resource CD.

Student Books

Problems and Practice (*Student Guide* Pages 431–434)
Fraction Chart from *Comparing Fractions* (*Student Guide* Page 336)

Teaching the Activity

Students solve the problems on the *Problems and Practice* Activity Pages in the *Student Guide* independently or in groups. Encourage students to use all the tools they used during mathematics class this year. They should show the strategies they use to find each solution.

A class discussion of the strategies students used to solve the problems provides a valuable review for the *End-of-Year Test*. This discussion will be helpful to those students who are experiencing difficulty with any of the concepts.

> **TIMS Tip**
>
> Review the problems before assigning them to students. If you have not completed all the units, choose the problems that are appropriate for your students.

Homework and Practice

Assign the *Problems and Practice* Activity Pages as homework.

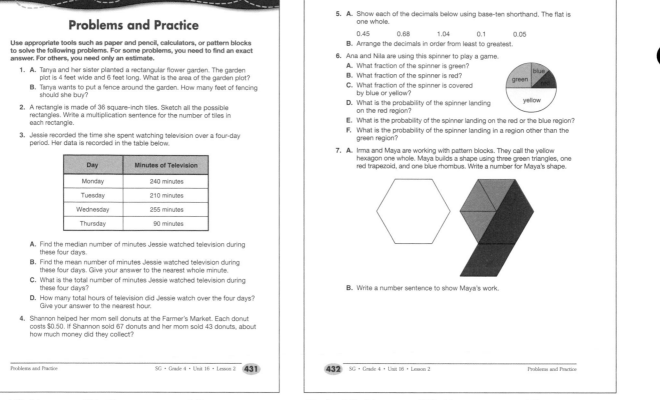

Student Guide - page 431 *(Answers on p. 44)*

Student Guide - page 432 *(Answers on p. 44)*

Problems and Practice

Use appropriate tools such as paper and pencil, calculators, or pattern blocks to solve the following problems. For some problems, you need to find an exact answer. For others, you need only an estimate.

1. A. Tanya and her sister planted a rectangular flower garden. The garden plot is 4 feet wide and 6 feet long. What is the area of the garden plot?
    B. Tanya wants to put a fence around the garden. How many feet of fencing should she buy?

2. A rectangle is made of 36 square-inch tiles. Sketch all the possible rectangles. Write a multiplication sentence for the number of tiles in each rectangle.

3. Jessie recorded the time she spent watching television over a four-day period. Her data is recorded in the table below.

Day	Minutes of Television
Monday	240 minutes
Tuesday	210 minutes
Wednesday	255 minutes
Thursday	90 minutes

   A. Find the median number of minutes Jessie watched television during these four days.
   B. Find the mean number of minutes Jessie watched television during these four days. Give your answer to the nearest whole minute.
   C. What is the total number of minutes Jessie watched television during these four days?
   D. How many total hours of television did Jessie watch over the four days? Give your answer to the nearest hour.

4. Shannon helped her mom sell donuts at the Farmer's Market. Each donut costs $0.50. If Shannon sold 67 donuts and her mom sold 43 donuts, about how much money did they collect?

5. A. Show each of the decimals below using base-ten shorthand. The flat is one whole.

   0.45   0.68   1.04   0.1   0.05

    B. Arrange the decimals in order from least to greatest.

6. Ana and Nila are using this spinner to play a game.
   A. What fraction of the spinner is green?
   B. What fraction of the spinner is red?
   C. What fraction of the spinner is covered by blue or yellow?
   D. What is the probability of the spinner landing on the red region?
   E. What is the probability of the spinner landing on the red or the blue region?
   F. What is the probability of the spinner landing in a region other than the green region?

7. A. Irma and Maya are working with pattern blocks. They call the yellow hexagon one whole. Maya builds a shape using three green triangles, one red trapezoid, and one blue rhombus. Write a number for Maya's shape.

    B. Write a number sentence to show Maya's work.

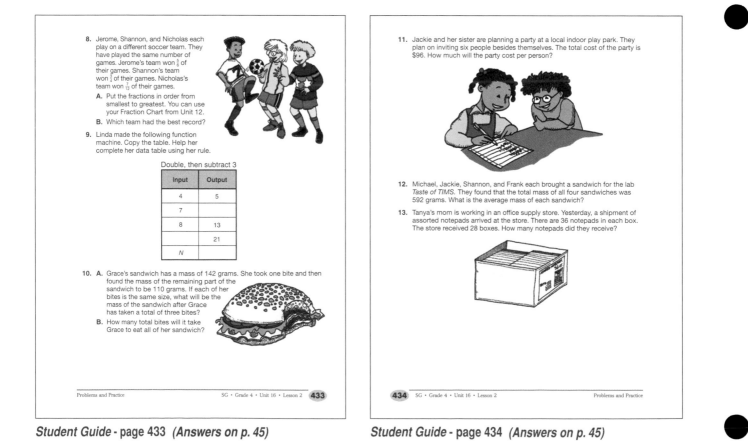

Student Guide - page 433 *(Answers on p. 45)*

Student Guide - page 434 *(Answers on p. 45)*

8. Jerome, Shannon, and Nicholas each play on a different soccer team. They have played the same number of games. Jerome's team won ⅝ of their games. Shannon's team won ⅔ of their games. Nicholas's team won 7/12 of their games.
   A. Put the fractions in order from smallest to greatest. You can use your Fraction Chart from Unit 12.
   B. Which team had the best record?

9. Linda made the following function machine. Copy the table. Help her complete her data table using her rule.

Double, then subtract 3

Input	Output
4	5
7	
8	13
	21
N	

10. A. Grace's sandwich has a mass of 142 grams. She took one bite and then found the mass of the remaining part of the sandwich to be 110 grams. If each of her bites is the same size, what will be the mass of the sandwich after Grace has taken a total of three bites?
    B. How many total bites will it take Grace to eat all of her sandwich?

11. Jackie and her sister are planning a party at a local indoor play park. They plan on inviting six people besides themselves. The total cost of the party is $96. How much will the party cost per person?

12. Michael, Jackie, Shannon, and Frank each brought a sandwich for the lab *Taste of TIMS*. They found that the total mass of all four sandwiches was 592 grams. What is the average mass of each sandwich?

13. Tanya's mom is working in an office supply store. Yesterday, a shipment of assorted notepads arrived at the store. There are 36 notepads in each box. The store received 28 boxes. How many notepads did they receive?

At a Glance

Teaching the Activity

1. Students complete the *Problems and Practice* Activity Pages in the *Student Guide* as homework or as an in-class review.

2. Students discuss the strategies used for solving each problem.

Homework

Assign the *Problems and Practice* Activity Pages.

Answer Key is on pages 44–45.

Notes:

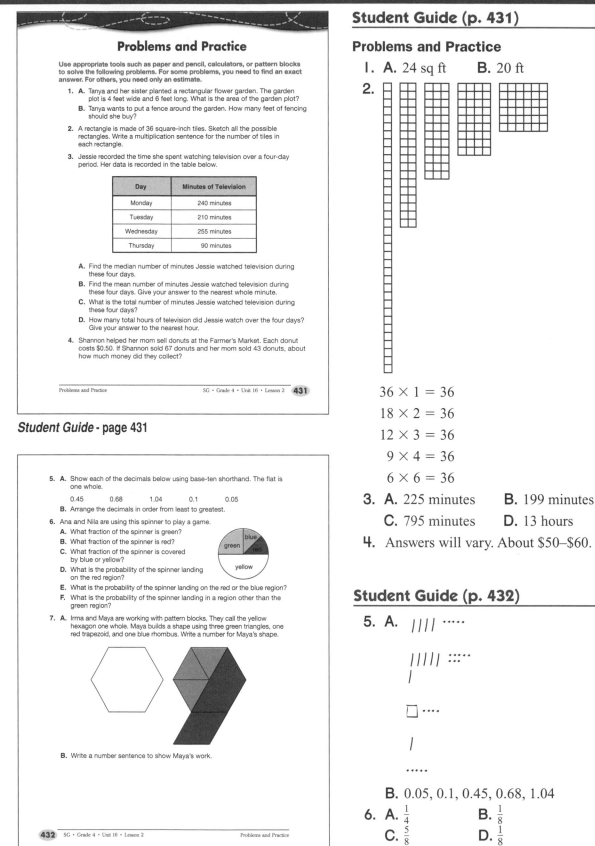

Problems and Practice

Use appropriate tools such as paper and pencil, calculators, or pattern blocks to solve the following problems. For some problems, you need to find an exact answer. For others, you need only an estimate.

1. **A.** Tanya and her sister planted a rectangular flower garden. The garden plot is 4 feet wide and 6 feet long. What is the area of the garden plot?

   B. Tanya wants to put a fence around the garden. How many feet of fencing should she buy?

2. A rectangle is made of 36 square-inch tiles. Sketch all the possible rectangles. Write a multiplication sentence for the number of tiles in each rectangle.

3. Jessie recorded the time she spent watching television over a four-day period. Her data is recorded in the table below.

Day	Minutes of Television
Monday	240 minutes
Tuesday	210 minutes
Wednesday	255 minutes
Thursday	90 minutes

   A. Find the median number of minutes Jessie watched television during these four days.

   B. Find the mean number of minutes Jessie watched television during these four days. Give your answer to the nearest whole minute.

   C. What is the total number of minutes Jessie watched television during these four days?

   D. How many total hours of television did Jessie watch over the four days? Give your answer to the nearest hour.

4. Shannon helped her mom sell donuts at the Farmer's Market. Each donut costs $0.50. If Shannon sold 67 donuts and her mom sold 43 donuts, about how much money did they collect?

Problems and Practice   SG • Grade 4 • Unit 16 • Lesson 2   **431**

Student Guide - page 431

5. **A.** Show each of the decimals below using base-ten shorthand. The flat is one whole.

   0.45   0.68   1.04   0.1   0.05

   B. Arrange the decimals in order from least to greatest.

6. Ana and Nila are using this spinner to play a game.

   A. What fraction of the spinner is green?

   B. What fraction of the spinner is red?

   C. What fraction of the spinner is covered by blue or yellow?

   D. What is the probability of the spinner landing on the red region?

   E. What is the probability of the spinner landing on the red or the blue region?

   F. What is the probability of the spinner landing in a region other than the green region?

7. **A.** Irma and Maya are working with pattern blocks. They call the yellow hexagon one whole. Maya builds a shape using three green triangles, one red trapezoid, and one blue rhombus. Write a number for Maya's shape.

   B. Write a number sentence to show Maya's work.

432   SG • Grade 4 • Unit 16 • Lesson 2   Problems and Practice

Student Guide - page 432

Student Guide (p. 431)

Problems and Practice

1. **A.** 24 sq ft   **B.** 20 ft

2.

$$36 \times 1 = 36$$
$$18 \times 2 = 36$$
$$12 \times 3 = 36$$
$$9 \times 4 = 36$$
$$6 \times 6 = 36$$

3. **A.** 225 minutes   **B.** 199 minutes

   C. 795 minutes   **D.** 13 hours

4. Answers will vary. About $50–$60.

Student Guide (p. 432)

5. **A.** ∥∥∥ ·····

   ∥∥∥∥ ::::··
   ∣

   ▢ ····

   ∣

   ·····

   B. 0.05, 0.1, 0.45, 0.68, 1.04

6. **A.** $\frac{1}{4}$ **B.** $\frac{1}{8}$

   C. $\frac{5}{8}$ **D.** $\frac{1}{8}$

   E. $\frac{1}{4}$ **F.** $\frac{3}{4}$

7. **A.** $1\frac{1}{3}$ or $\frac{4}{3}$

   B. $\frac{3}{6} + \frac{1}{2} + \frac{1}{3} = 1\frac{1}{3}$ or $\frac{4}{3}$

Student Guide (p. 433)

8. A. $\frac{7}{12}, \frac{3}{4}, \frac{5}{6}$

B. Jerome's team

9.

Double, then subtract 3

Input	Output
4	5
7	11
8	13
12	21
N	$2 \times N - 3$

10. A. 46 g

B. 5 bites

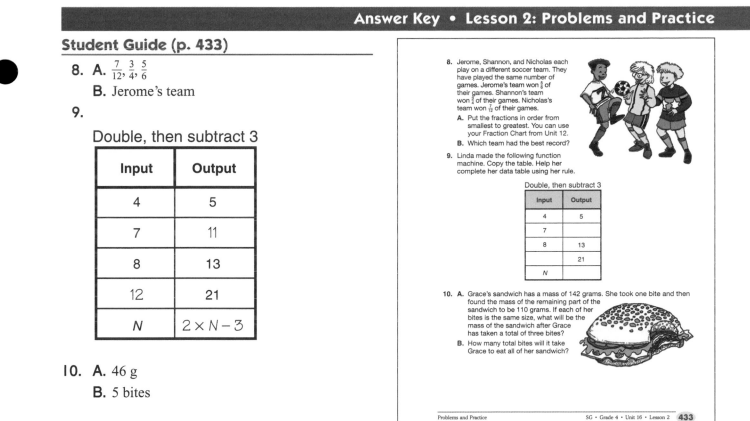

Student Guide - page 433

Student Guide (p. 434)

11. $12

12. 148 g

13. 1008 notepads

Student Guide - page 434

Lesson 3

Area vs. Length

Lesson Overview

Estimated Class Sessions
3

Students use the TIMS Laboratory Method to investigate the relationship between area and length for rectangles of fixed width. This lab is appropriate for inclusion in students' portfolios to document students' progress in using the TIMS Laboratory Method throughout the year.

Key Content

- Measuring length in inches.
- Finding the area of rectangles.
- Collecting, organizing, graphing, and analyzing data.
- Making and interpreting point graphs.
- Identifying and using variables.
- Using patterns in tables and graphs to make predictions.
- Communicating solution strategies verbally and in writing.

Key Vocabulary

- area
- length
- variable
- width

Math Facts

DPP Bit C provides practice with division facts.

Homework

Students complete Parts 7 and 8 of the Home Practice.

Assessment

1. Use the *TIMS Multidimensional Rubric* or a point scale to assess students' abilities to implement the steps of the TIMS Laboratory Method.
2. Assess students' letters to Myrna using the Telling dimension of the *TIMS Multidimensional Rubric*.
3. Use the *Observational Assessment Record* to document students' abilities to collect, organize, graph, and analyze data.

Curriculum Sequence

Before This Unit

Students have completed several labs in which they used point graphs to represent and analyze the data: Unit 2 *Perimeter vs. Length,* Unit 5 *Bouncing Ball,* Unit 8 *Volume vs. Number,* Unit 10 *Downhill Racer,* and Unit 15 *Taste of TIMS.*

Materials List

Supplies and Copies

Student	Teacher
Supplies for Each Student • ruler **Supplies for Each Student Group** • 50 square-inch tiles	**Supplies**
Copies • 1 copy of *Three-column Data Table* per student (*Unit Resource Guide* Page 59) • 1 copy of *Centimeter Graph Paper* per student (*Unit Resource Guide* Page 60)	**Copies/Transparencies** • 1 copy of *TIMS Multidimensional Rubric* (*Teacher Implementation Guide,* Assessment section) • 1 transparency or poster of Student Rubric: *Telling* (*Teacher Implementation Guide,* Assessment section)

All blackline masters including assessment, transparency, and DPP masters are also on the Teacher Resource CD.

Student Books

Area vs. Length (*Student Guide* Pages 435–438)
Student Rubric: *Telling* (*Student Guide* Appendix C and Inside Back Cover)

Daily Practice and Problems and Home Practice

DPP items C–H (*Unit Resource Guide* Pages 14–16)
Home Practice Parts 7–8 (*Discovery Assignment Book* Page 250)

Note: Classrooms whose pacing differs significantly from the suggested pacing of the units should use the Math Facts Calendar in Section 4 of the *Facts Resource Guide* to ensure students receive the complete math facts program.

Assessment Tools

Observational Assessment Record (*Unit Resource Guide* Pages 9–10)
TIMS Multidimensional Rubric (*Teacher Implementation Guide,* Assessment section)

Daily Practice and Problems

Suggestions for using the DPPs are on page 55.

C. Bit: Division Fact Practice (URG p. 14) $\boxed{\frac{5}{\times 7}}$

1. A. $50 \div 5 =$ B. $12 \div 3 =$
   C. $90 \div 10 =$ D. $0 \div 8 =$
   E. $24 \div 8 =$ F. $28 \div 7 =$
   G. $56 \div 8 =$ H. $80 \div 8 =$
   I. $4 \div 4 =$ J. $48 \div 8 =$
2. Explain your strategy for Question 1G.

F. Task: More Area and Perimeter (URG p. 15)

A rectangle is 4 cm wide. Its length is twice as long as its width.

1. Draw this rectangle. You may use a piece of *Centimeter Grid Paper*.
2. What is the area of the rectangle?
3. What is the perimeter of the rectangle?

D. Task: Rounding Numbers (URG p. 14) $\boxed{\text{N}}$

1. Order the numbers below from smallest to largest.

   A. 780,188   B. 708,589
   C. 89,524   D. 190,776
   E. 17,460   F. 4,239,454

2. Find at least two ways to round each of the numbers above.

G. Bit: Fractions (URG p. 16) $\boxed{\text{N}}$

Which is larger:

A. $\frac{1}{12}$ or $\frac{1}{10}$?   B. $\frac{3}{2}$ or $1\frac{1}{4}$?

C. $\frac{6}{12}$ or 0.5?   D. $\frac{5}{8}$ or 0.4?

Be prepared to explain how you decided on your answers.

E. Bit: Area and Perimeter (URG p. 15)

1. What is the area of the rectangle below?

2 inches

3 inches

2. What is the perimeter?

H. Challenge: Solving Problems (URG p. 16)

1. A tailor spent half his money on cotton cloth and half on wool cloth. He bought 10 yards of cotton and 2 yards of wool. The cotton cost $2 per yard. How much was the wool per yard?
2. An art teacher has to order construction paper for next year. She ordered 300 packages of construction paper. Each of the 15 primary-grade classes needs 12 packages of paper for the entire school year. The rest of the paper is evenly shared among the 10 intermediate-grade classes. How many packages do each of the intermediate classes receive?

Since *Area vs. Length* is an assessment lab, we recommend that students complete it with little teacher input. This will provide an indication of their abilities to tackle and solve problems on their own. Have students work in small groups to complete some parts of this lab and work independently to complete other parts. Students work in small groups to draw their pictures, collect their data, and make their graphs. Then they work independently to complete the discussion questions and write letters to Myrna.

By including this lab in their portfolios, students can look for growth in their abilities to collect, organize, and graph data as well as use the data to solve problems. Compare student work on other labs, including the *Perimeter vs. Length* lab from Unit 2 and *Volume vs. Number* in Unit 8. Have students add information about this lab to the *Experiment Review Chart* from Lesson 1.

Part 1 Defining the Variables and Drawing the Picture

Read and discuss the first page of the *Area vs. Length* Lab Pages in the *Student Guide*. This initial discussion should be straightforward. *Questions 1–2* ask students to look at the *Perimeter vs. Length* lab to remind themselves of the type of planes they studied and the variables in the lab. This time, students will study the variables' area and length rather than perimeter and length. Note that in both labs, the two main variables are numerical variables.

Assign each group one type of plane with the given runway width: light plane (width = 1 in), commuter plane (width = 2 in), short-haul jet (width = 3 in), long-haul jet (width = 4 in), or heavy-transport planes (width = 5 in). (The groups with the heavy-transport planes will need 50 square-inch tiles. If you have a limited supply of tiles, the groups building runways for heavy-transport planes will need more tiles than the other groups.) For each group, the runway width and the type of plane are fixed.

After you discuss the lab and are confident that students understand the procedure, ask them to draw pictures of the investigation *(Question 3)*. Emphasize that a good picture shows the equipment, identifies the variables, and communicates the procedures. An example of a student drawing is shown in Figure 2. Note that the square-inch tiles, the type of plane, the width, and the variables (*A* for the area of the runway and *L* for its length) are clear in the picture.

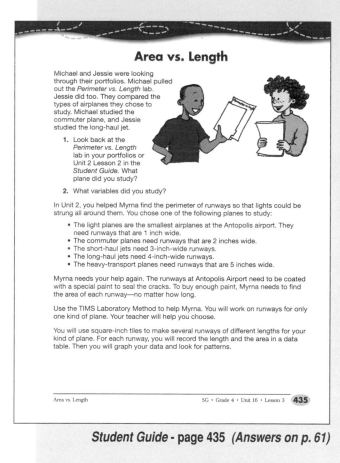

Area vs. Length

Michael and Jessie were looking through their portfolios. Michael pulled out the *Perimeter vs. Length* lab. Jessie did too. They compared the types of airplanes they chose to study. Michael studied the commuter plane, and Jessie studied the long-haul jet.

1. Look back at the *Perimeter vs. Length* lab in your portfolios or Unit 2 Lesson 2 in the *Student Guide*. What plane did you study?

2. What variables did you study?

In Unit 2, you helped Myrna find the perimeter of runways so that lights could be strung all around them. You chose one of the following planes to study:

- The light planes are the smallest airplanes at the Antopolis airport. They need runways that are 1 inch wide.
- The commuter planes need runways that are 2 inches wide.
- The short-haul jets need 3-inch-wide runways.
- The long-haul jets need 4-inch-wide runways.
- The heavy-transport planes need runways that are 5 inches wide.

Myrna needs your help again. The runways at Antopolis Airport need to be coated with a special paint to seal the cracks. To buy enough paint, Myrna needs to find the area of each runway—no matter how long.

Use the TIMS Laboratory Method to help Myrna. You will work on runways for only one kind of plane. Your teacher will help you choose.

You will use square-inch tiles to make several runways of different lengths for your kind of plane. For each runway, you will record the length and the area in a data table. Then you will graph your data and look for patterns.

Area vs. Length   SG • Grade 4 • Unit 16 • Lesson 3   **435**

Student Guide - page 435 (Answers on p. 61)

Draw

3. Draw a picture of the lab. Be sure to show the two main variables, Length (*L*) and Area (*A*). Also show your kind of airplane and how wide your runways will be.

You will use square-inch tiles to make several runways for your kind of airplane. With your group, decide how long to make your runways. Do not make runways longer than 10 inches or you may have trouble graphing your data.

Collect

4. Make your runways. Record the length and area of each runway. Keep track of your data in a table like the one shown here.

Runway Data Table for _____ (Type of Plane)
Width = _____

W Width of Runway (in inches)	L Length of Runway (in inches)	A Area of Runway (in square inches)

436 SG • Grade 4 • Unit 16 • Lesson 3   Area vs. Length

Student Guide - page 436 (Answers on p. 61)

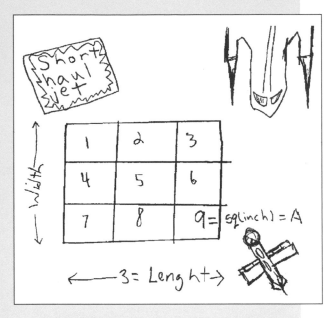

Figure 2: *A student's picture of the lab*

Part 2 Collecting and Organizing the Data

Students are asked to choose different lengths for their particular runway (light plane, short-haul, or commuter, etc.). The width is held fixed. Then students build each runway with square-inch tiles and find its area. Students should limit their runway lengths to 10 inches. This will keep them from running out of tiles and make graphing the data easier.

Students record their data in a *Three-column Data Table (Question 4).* As the data accumulates, they should study their tables to see if there are any patterns. Figure 3 shows sample student data for short-haul jets.

Question 5 asks students to identify the variables. The length (L) of the runways is the manipulated variable since students choose these values. Area (A) is the responding variable since they find the areas as a result of the investigation. The width (W) of the rectangles is the fixed variable and does not change for each type of plane.

Part 3 Graphing the Data

Try to give students as little help as possible with the graphing so you can better assess their skills. If the data points for this lab do not fall right on the line, there is either a problem with the data or with the graph. Students label and scale their axes, plot their points, and fit a line to those points *(Questions 6–7).*

Runway Data Table for ___Short-Haul Jets___
(Type of Plane)

Width = ___3 inches___

W Width of Runway (in inches)	L Length of Runway (in inches)	A Area of Runway (in square inches)
3	5	15
3	6	18
3	7	21
3	9	27
3	10	30

Figure 3: *Short-haul jet runway data*

Part 4 Exploring the Data

For *Questions 9* and *10,* students find the areas of a 4-inch-long runway and a 12-inch-long runway. Some may use their data tables while others count each square inch to find the area. Some may count how many tiles are in one row and then repeatedly add that number. Others will discover that the length multiplied by the width yields the area. Still others may use the graph to answer the question. All are appropriate strategies to find the answer. Remind students to show how they found their answers.

To answer *Question 12,* students must give a general rule for finding the area of a runway, not just an example. Possible responses follow:

* *Area equals length times the width.*
* *Area = Length × Width*
* *A = L × W*

Question 13 asks the difference between inches and square inches. If students have difficulty answering this question, ask:

* *When are inches used?*
* *When are square inches used?*
* *What is the difference between them?*

See Figure 5 for a sample student response to *Question 13.* This student shows an understanding of the difference between linear and area measurement.

> That a inch is just like this ⎯ and a squure is like this ☐ thats what is diffent of them

Figure 5: *A student's response to* **Question 13**

Part 5 Writing Letters to Myrna

Review the TIMS Student Rubric: *Telling* before students write their letters to Myrna *(Question 15).* Discuss characteristics of good and poor letters, perhaps using examples from letters your students wrote for *Perimeter vs. Length.* Alternatively, you might use the actual student letters on the following page as examples that fall short of what is desired.

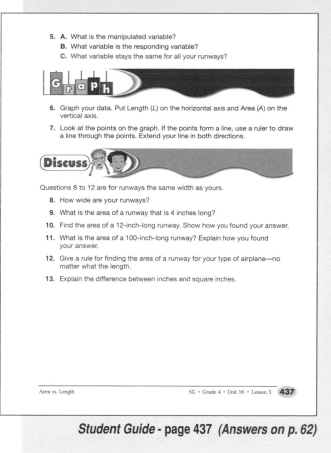

5. **A.** What is the manipulated variable?
   B. What variable is the responding variable?
   C. What variable stays the same for all your runways?

6. Graph your data. Put Length (*L*) on the horizontal axis and Area (*A*) on the vertical axis.

7. Look at the points on the graph. If the points form a line, use a ruler to draw a line through the points. Extend your line in both directions.

Questions 8 to 12 are for runways the same width as yours.

8. How wide are your runways?
9. What is the area of a runway that is 4 inches long?
10. Find the area of a 12-inch-long runway. Show how you found your answer.
11. What is the area of a 100-inch-long runway? Explain how you found your answer.
12. Give a rule for finding the area of a runway for your type of airplane—no matter what the length.
13. Explain the difference between inches and square inches.

Area vs. Length   SG • Grade 4 • Unit 16 • Lesson 3   **437**

Student Guide - page 437 (Answers on p. 62)

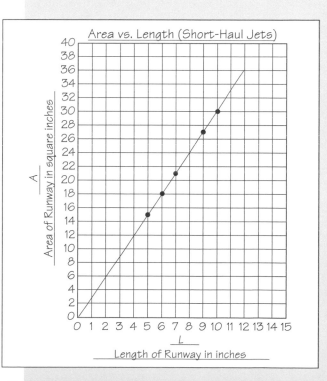

Figure 4: *A student graph of the area of short-haul jet runways with a fixed width of 3 inches*

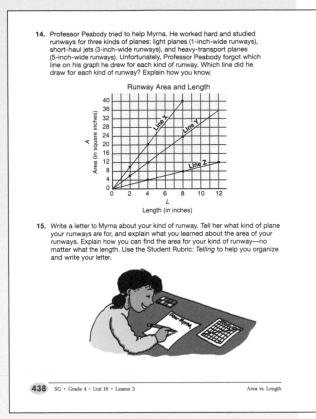

14. Professor Peabody tried to help Myrna. He worked hard and studied runways for three kinds of planes: light planes (1-inch-wide runways), short-haul jets (3-inch-wide runways), and heavy-transport planes (5-inch-wide runways). Unfortunately, Professor Peabody forgot which line on his graph he drew for each kind of runway. Which line did he draw for each kind of runway? Explain how you know.

Runway Area and Length

15. Write a letter to Myrna about your kind of runway. Tell her what kind of plane your runways are for, and explain what you learned about the area of your runways. Explain how you can find the area for your kind of runway—no matter what the length. Use the Student Rubric: *Telling* to help you organize and write your letter.

Student Guide - page 438 *(Answers on p. 62)*

> Dear Myrna, My runways are for heavy transport planes. I learned that you'd get a big area just using a heavy transport plane and length 10 inches. How you can find the area The lines in the runway always stay the same

> Dear Mara Mrmdon, My runway is for the light hul plain I learned that it could be a little runway or a big runway. I counted the square all four sides. My runway is a little runway for the light hul plain.

> Dear myran, my runway is the Short Halu Jet runway. It is 3 inches long and 3 inches wide. My plane would be the short haul jet plane. I learned how to cont the area of my runway. I learned that it dose not take a long time. It did not take me a long time.

The first letter above mentions the type of plane but little else that is relevant and correct. The other letters include the type of plane and identify counting as one strategy for finding the area, but are unclear about what is being counted. All these letters would be scored at Level 1 on the *TIMS Multidimensional Rubric*.

When grading your students' letters, comment on the first drafts and give them an opportunity to revise their letters before you assign scores. To assist you in scoring students' work, questions specific to this task for the Telling dimension of the *TIMS Multidimensional Rubric* are listed below.

Telling

* Did they include the type of plane?
* Did they clearly describe how they could find the area for any rectangle?
* Did they use units such as inches and square inches properly?
* Did they clearly explain the use of any pictures, data tables, and symbols?

Two more samples of student responses to *Question 15* are shown. These students have been given scores on the Telling dimension of the *TIMS Multidimensional Rubric*. Following the scores, you will find examples of the notations teachers made on the *TIMS Multidimensional Rubric* to score the papers (Figures 6 and 7).

Student work from Martin:

Dear Myrna, My runway is for the heavy transport. What I learned about area is that it is a inche in a sertain shape. Like a square. It is for any shape. But the length does matter. It is important for the area. When the length is big the area is big. Same thing with small length. How you can find the area of my runway is to count the inches in it. But if you can't count you have to multiply the length with the width. If you know the length. Why I solved it this way was because I though it was the smart way to do it. I think that if you aren't lazy you will think good. But that does-n't mean your lazy. Our work here was just like perimeter vs. length. Your friend, Martin.
[Note: Martin included a picture.]

Telling score: 3

Martin's description is fairly clear and complete. He specifies the type of plane and states that when the length changes, the area also changes. He notes that, although it is sometimes a good way to find the area, counting is not always practical. In this case, Martin generalizes to finding the area of a rectangle by multi-plying the length and the width. Martin ends his letter by mentioning his work with *Perimeter vs. Length,* although he did not specify how the two labs are simi-lar. Martin's first several sentences, however, are con-fusing and indicate that he might not understand the idea of measuring area using square units. Overall, Martin has done a good, though not outstanding, job of communicating what he learned in this lab. See Figure 6.

Telling	Level 4	Level 3	Level 2	Level 1
Includes response with an explanation and/or description which is...	Complete and clear	Fairly complete and clear	Perhaps ambiguous or unclear	Totally unclear or irrelevant
Presents supporting arguments which are...	Strong and sound	Logically sound, but may contain minor gaps	Incomplete or logically unsound	Not present
Uses pictures, symbols, tables, and graphs which are...	Correct and clearly relevant	Present with minor errors or some-what irrelevant	Present with errors and/or irrelevant	Not present or completely inappropriate
Uses terminology...	Clearly and precisely	With minor errors	With major errors	Not at all

Figure 6: *Scoring Martin's communication skills on **Question 15** using the* TIMS Multidimensional Rubric

Student work from James:

Dear Myrna, How are you doing at Antopolis airport. Well I'm here to help you on the area of the runways. Our kind of runway is seven inches long and five inches wide. The area of or runway is 35. Our runway is for the heavy transport and I learned that area means to count the boxs. I also learned that an area of 100 inches long is 500. You can find it by doing counting so you can multiply 7 X 5 = 35 or your can just count the boxes to get 35. Well Myrna now you know how to do the area of those runways right. Theres just one more thing I hope you can read this o.k. o.k.. Love, James

Telling score: 2

James specifies the type of plane. He also uses units appropriately for length and width, although he stops using them later on and never uses square inches. Rather than giving a general rule for finding the area of any runway, James gives an example of a 5-inch by 7-inch runway. He gives two strategies for finding the area of this rectangle (counting and multiplying), but fails to generalize to runways of arbitrary length. James's letter falls short of what is desired. See Figure 7.

Telling	Level 4	Level 3	Level 2	Level 1
Includes response with an explanation and/or description which is…	Complete and clear	Fairly complete and clear	Perhaps ambiguous or unclear	Totally unclear or irrelevant
Presents supporting arguments which are…	Strong and sound	Logically sound, but may contain minor gaps	Incomplete or logically unsound	Not present
Uses pictures, symbols, tables, and graphs which are…	Correct and clearly relevant	Present with minor errors or somewhat irrelevant	Present with errors and/or irrelevant	Not present or completely inappropriate
Uses terminology…	Clearly and precisely	With minor errors	With major errors	Not at all

Figure 7: *Scoring James's communication skills on* **Question 15** *using the* TIMS Multidimensional Rubric

Math Facts

DPP Bit C provides practice with division facts.

Homework and Practice

- DPP Task D asks students to round and order large numbers. Items E and F review area and perimeter. Bit G compares fractions and decimals. Challenge H is a word problem with several steps.

- Assign Parts 7 and 8 of the Home Practice.

Answers for Parts 7 and 8 of the Home Practice are in the Answer Key at the end of this lesson and at the end of this unit.

Assessment

Options for Grading the Lab

There are many valid alternatives for scoring students' papers. Some options are listed here.

- Use the *TIMS Multidimensional Rubric* to score certain parts of the lab. The letter to Myrna is particularly suitable for this. This option is discussed in Part 5 of the Lesson Guide.

- Divide the lab into parts (e.g., picture, data collection, graph, and questions) and use a point system to grade each part. Points can be assigned based on the following criteria:

Drawing the Picture

1. Did the student draw at least one runway with the correct width?
2. Are the variables (length, *L,* area, *A,* and width, *W*) labeled correctly?
3. Did the student identify the type of plane he or she is studying?

Collecting and Recording Data

1. Are the columns in the data table labeled with length *(L),* width *(W),* and area *(A)?*
2. Are inches and square inches included in the data table?
3. Are the areas correct for each chosen length?

Graphing the Data

1. Does the graph have a title?
2. Are the axes labeled and scaled appropriately?
3. Are the points plotted correctly?
4. Did the student use a ruler to draw a line through the points?

Name _____ Date _____

PART 7 Function Machines

1. Complete the following tables.

A.

Input N	Output $3 + 2 \times N$
1	5
2	
3	
4	
5	
6	
7	
8	

B.

Input N	Output $5 \times N$
1	5
2	
3	
4	
5	
6	
7	
8	

2. Nicholas predicted that the outputs would be the same for both data tables. Are they the same? Why or why not?

PART 8 Downhill Racer

You will need a piece of *Centimeter Graph Paper.*

1. John rolled a car down a ramp at three different heights. At each height he took three trials. The data here shows the average distance (in cm) the car rolled at each height. Graph the data on *Centimeter Graph Paper.*

2. If the points form a line, fit a line to the points.

3. Predict the distance the car will roll if the height of the ramp is 30 cm.

Downhill Racer

Height (in cm)	Average Distance (in cm)
8	100
16	198
24	305

250 DAB • Grade 4 • Unit 16   ASSESSING OUR LEARNING

Discovery Assignment Book - page 250 (Answers on p. 63)

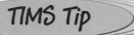
Solving the Problems

1. Are the answers correct based on the data?
2. Did the student give complete explanations for his or her answers?

- Observe students as they work in their groups to note their abilities to collect, organize, graph, and analyze data. Record your observations on the *Observational Assessment Record*.

These alternatives are not mutually exclusive. You might, for example, score part of the lab using points and score other parts using the *TIMS Multi-dimensional Rubric*.

Include this lab in each student's portfolio. They can compare their work on this lab to previously completed labs already in their portfolios. Lesson 6 *Portfolios* provides a structure for such a self-assessment.

Extension

After students complete **Question 14,** graph all five types of planes on an overhead transparency using colored pens. (See Figure 8.) Ask students what they notice about the graph. Some may notice that all the lines start at the point, $L = 0$ in and $A = 0$ sq in, and that all are straight lines that go "uphill." The lines for the wider runways have steeper slopes.

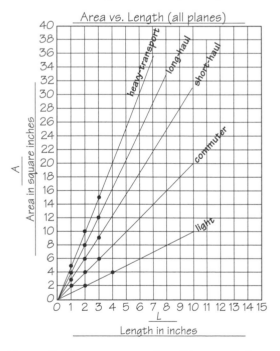

Figure 8: *Runway areas for all types of planes*

Math Facts and Daily Practice and Problems

DPP Bit C provides practice with division facts. Task D develops number sense with large numbers. Items E and F review area and perimeter. DPP item G compares fractions and decimals, and item H is a word problem.

Part 1. Defining the Variables and Drawing the Picture

1. Use the *Student Guide* story of the Antopolis Airport on the *Area vs. Length* Lab Pages to:
   - Remind students of the *Perimeter vs. Length* lab in Unit 2 *(Questions 1–2)*.
   - Pose the question for this lab, "How can you find the area of a runway of any length?"
   - Identify the key variables—Length (*L*), Width (*W*), and Area (*A*).
2. Students draw pictures of the lab *(Question 3)*. The pictures should identify the key variables and show the width of the runways they are studying.

Part 2. Collecting and Organizing the Data

1. Students decide how long to make their runways. The maximum length should be 10 inches.
2. Students use square-inch tiles to build runways of fixed width and varying length, recording *L*, *W*, and *A* in their data tables. *(Question 4)*
3. Students identify the manipulated, responding, and fixed variables in the investigation. *(Question 5)*

Part 3. Graphing the Data

1. Students draw point graphs of their data. *(Question 6)*
2. Students fit lines to the points on their graphs. *(Question 7)*

Part 4. Exploring the Data

Students answer *Questions 8–14* in the *Area vs. Length* Assessment Lab Pages in the *Student Guide.*

Part 5. Writing Letters to Myrna

1. Review the TIMS Student Rubric: *Telling.*
2. Students write letters to Myrna *(Question 15)*. They must explain how to find the area of their kind of runway, no matter what the length.
3. Students include this lab in their collection folders.

At a Glance

Homework

Students complete Parts 7 and 8 of the Home Practice.

Assessment

1. Use the *TIMS Multidimensional Rubric* or a point scale to assess students' abilities to implement the steps of the TIMS Laboratory Method.
2. Assess students' letters to Myrna using the Telling dimension of the *TIMS Multidimensional Rubric*.
3. Use the *Observational Assessment Record* to document students' abilities to collect, organize, graph, and analyze data.

Extension

After *Question 14,* graph all types of planes on a transparency. Ask students what they know about the graph.

Answer Key is on pages 61–63.

Notes:

Name _____ Date _____

_____

Three-column Data Table, Blackline Master

Name _____   Date _____

Centimeter Graph Paper, Blackline Master

Student Guide (p. 435)

Area vs. Length

1. Answers will vary.

2. Perimeter, length*

Area vs. Length

Michael and Jessie were looking through their portfolios. Michael pulled out the *Perimeter vs. Length* lab. Jessie did too. They compared the types of airplanes they chose to study. Michael studied the commuter plane, and Jessie studied the long-haul jet.

1. Look back at the *Perimeter vs. Length* lab in your portfolios or Unit 2 Lesson 2 in the *Student Guide*. What plane did you study?

2. What variables did you study?

In Unit 2, you helped Myrna find the perimeter of runways so that lights could be strung all around them. You chose one of the following planes to study:

- The light planes are the smallest airplanes at the Antopolis airport. They need runways that are 1 inch wide.
- The commuter planes need runways that are 2 inches wide.
- The short-haul jets need 3-inch-wide runways.
- The long-haul jets need 4-inch-wide runways.
- The heavy-transport planes need runways that are 5 inches wide.

Myrna needs your help again. The runways at Antopolis Airport need to be coated with a special paint to seal the cracks. To buy enough paint, Myrna needs to find the area of each runway—no matter how long.

Use the TIMS Laboratory Method to help Myrna. You will work on runways for only one kind of plane. Your teacher will help you choose.

You will use square-inch tiles to make several runways of different lengths for your kind of plane. For each runway, you will record the length and the area in a data table. Then you will graph your data and look for patterns.

Area vs. Length   SG • Grade 4 • Unit 16 • Lesson 3   **435**

Student Guide - page 435

Student Guide (p. 436)

3. See Figure 2 in Lesson Guide 3 for a sample student picture.*

4. See Figure 3 in Lesson Guide 3 for a sample data table.*

Draw

3. Draw a picture of the lab. Be sure to show the two main variables, Length (*L*) and Area (*A*). Also show your kind of airplane and how wide your runways will be.

You will use square-inch tiles to make several runways for your kind of airplane. With your group, decide how long to make your runways. Do not make runways longer than 10 inches or you may have trouble graphing your data.

Collect

4. Make your runways. Record the length and area of each runway. Keep track of your data in a table like the one shown here.

Runway Data Table for _____
                              (Type of Plane)
         Width = _____

W Width of Runway (in inches)	L Length of Runway (in inches)	A Area of Runway (in square inches)

436 SG • Grade 4 • Unit 16 • Lesson 3   Area vs. Length

Student Guide - page 436

*Answers and/or discussion are included in the Lesson Guide.

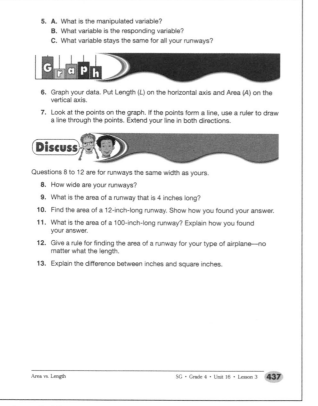

Student Guide - page 437

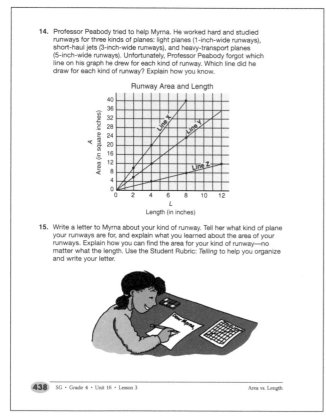

Student Guide - page 438

*Answers and/or discussion are included in the Lesson Guide.

Student Guide (p. 437)

5. * **A.** Length of runways (L)

    B. Area of runways (A)

    C. width

6. See Figure 4 in Lesson Guide 3 for a sample graph.*

7. See Figure 4 in Lesson Guide 3 for a sample graph.*

8. Answers will vary.

9. Answers will vary based on the width of the runways.*

10. Answers will vary based on the width of the runways.*

11. Answers will vary based on the width of the runways.*

12. Area = Length × Width. Students may express the relationship in various ways.*

13. Inches are used to measure length and have only one dimension. Square inches are used to measure area and have two dimensions. See Figure 5 in Lesson Guide 3 for a sample student response.*

Student Guide (p. 438)

14. Line X is for heavy transports. Line Y is for short-haul jets. Line Z is for light planes.

15. See Lesson Guide 3 for a detailed discussion of scoring students' letters.*

Discovery Assignment Book (p. 250)

Home Practice*

Part 7. Function Machines

I. A.

Input N	Output 3 + 2 × N
1	5
2	7
3	9
4	11
5	13
6	15
7	17
8	19

B.

Input N	Output 5 × N
1	5
2	10
3	15
4	20
5	25
6	30
7	35
8	40

2. No, the outputs are not the same. If the order of operations is followed correctly in Table A, the number (N) is multiplied by 2 first, then the 3 is added.

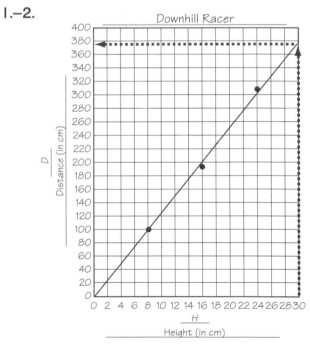

Name _____ Date _____

PART 7 Function Machines
1. Complete the following tables.

A.

Input N	Output 3 + 2 × N
1	5
2	
3	
4	
5	
6	
7	
8	

B.

Input N	Output 5 × N
1	5
2	
3	
4	
5	
6	
7	
8	

2. Nicholas predicted that the outputs would be the same for both data tables. Are they the same? Why or why not?

PART 8 Downhill Racer
You will need a piece of *Centimeter Graph Paper.*

1. John rolled a car down a ramp at three different heights. At each height he took three trials. The data here shows the average distance (in cm) the car rolled at each height. Graph the data on *Centimeter Graph Paper.*

2. If the points form a line, fit a line to the points.

3. Predict the distance the car will roll if the height of the ramp is 30 cm.

Downhill Racer

Height (in cm)	Average Distance (in cm)
8	100
16	198
24	305

250 DAB • Grade 4 • Unit 16   ASSESSING OUR LEARNING

Discovery Assignment Book - page 250

Part 8. Downhill Racer

I.–2.

3. Answers will vary. The graph above shows $D = 375$ cm when $H = 30$. Accept answers between 340 and 410 cm.

*Answers for all the Home Practice in the *Discovery Assignment Book* are at the end of the unit.

Lesson 4

The Many-Eyed Dragonfly

Lesson Overview

Estimated Class Sessions

2

Students determine the growth pattern of a Many-Eyed Dragonfly, a creature on the imaginary planet Gzorp as introduced in Unit 15 Lesson 3. Creatures on Gzorp are made up of squares and grow according to carefully defined rules. Students use the pattern to determine what the Many-Eyed Dragonfly will look like at various ages. Students write about their solutions.

Key Content

- Identifying patterns.
- Extending number patterns.
- Connecting geometric patterns and number patterns.
- Using patterns to make predictions and solve problems.
- Solving open-response problems and communicating problem-solving strategies.

Math Facts

DPP Bit I provides practice with math facts.

Homework

Assign Parts 3 and 4 of the Home Practice.

Assessment

Use the Solving, Knowing, and Telling dimensions of the *TIMS Multidimensional Rubric* to assess student work on *The Many-Eyed Dragonfly* Assessment Blackline Masters.

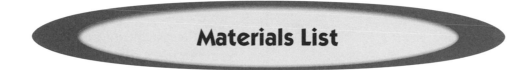

Curriculum Sequence

Before This Unit

Students have solved open-response problems throughout fourth grade. They used the student rubrics to guide them as they solved the problems and wrote about their solutions. For specific examples, see Unit 2 Lesson 3, Unit 5 Lesson 6, Unit 7 Lesson 3, Unit 8 Lesson 5, Unit 10 Lesson 3, and Unit 12 Lesson 8. In particular, to assess growth in students' abilities to solve problems and communicate solution strategies, compare each

student's work in this lesson to that in Unit 2 Lesson 3 *Letter to Myrna* and Unit 8 Lesson 5 *Hour Walk.*

In Unit 15, students were introduced to the imaginary planet Gzorp and the creatures who live there. While these problems use planet Gzorp as their setting, completion of Unit 15 is not necessary for students to solve the problems.

Materials List

Supplies and Copies

Student	Teacher
Supplies for Each Student • square-inch tiles • calculator	**Supplies**
Copies • 1 copy of *The Many-Eyed Dragonfly* per student (*Unit Resource Guide* Pages 77–80) • 1 copy of *Two-column Data Table* per student (*Unit Resource Guide* Page 81)	**Copies/Transparencies** • 1 transparency or poster of Student Rubrics: *Knowing, Solving,* and *Telling* (*Teacher Implementation Guide,* Assessment section) • 1 copy of *TIMS Multidimensional Rubric* (*Teacher Implementation Guide,* Assessment section)

All blackline masters including assessment, transparency, and DPP masters are also on the Teacher Resource CD.

Student Books

Student Rubrics: *Knowing, Solving,* and *Telling* (*Student Guide* Appendix A, B, and C and Inside Back Cover)

Daily Practice and Problems and Home Practice

DPP items I–L (*Unit Resource Guide* Pages 17–18)
Home Practice Parts 3–4 (*Discovery Assignment Book* Page 248)

Note: Classrooms whose pacing differs significantly from the suggested pacing of the units should use the Math Facts Calendar in Section 4 of the *Facts Resource Guide* to ensure students receive the complete math facts program.

Assessment Tools

TIMS Multidimensional Rubric (*Teacher Implementation Guide,* Assessment section)

Daily Practice and Problems

Suggestions for using the DPPs are on page 70.

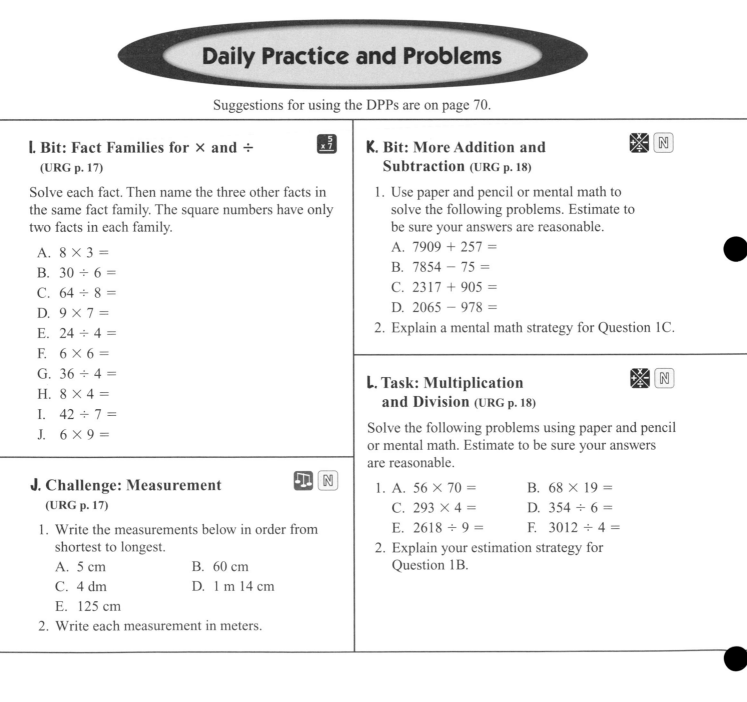

I. Bit: Fact Families for × and ÷ $\boxed{\frac{5}{\times 7}}$
(URG p. 17)

Solve each fact. Then name the three other facts in the same fact family. The square numbers have only two facts in each family.

A. $8 \times 3 =$

B. $30 \div 6 =$

C. $64 \div 8 =$

D. $9 \times 7 =$

E. $24 \div 4 =$

F. $6 \times 6 =$

G. $36 \div 4 =$

H. $8 \times 4 =$

I. $42 \div 7 =$

J. $6 \times 9 =$

J. Challenge: Measurement
(URG p. 17)

1. Write the measurements below in order from shortest to longest.

   A. 5 cm   B. 60 cm

   C. 4 dm   D. 1 m 14 cm

   E. 125 cm

2. Write each measurement in meters.

K. Bit: More Addition and Subtraction (URG p. 18)

1. Use paper and pencil or mental math to solve the following problems. Estimate to be sure your answers are reasonable.

   A. $7909 + 257 =$

   B. $7854 - 75 =$

   C. $2317 + 905 =$

   D. $2065 - 978 =$

2. Explain a mental math strategy for Question 1C.

L. Task: Multiplication and Division (URG p. 18)

Solve the following problems using paper and pencil or mental math. Estimate to be sure your answers are reasonable.

1. A. $56 \times 70 =$ B. $68 \times 19 =$

   C. $293 \times 4 =$ D. $354 \div 6 =$

   E. $2618 \div 9 =$ F. $3012 \div 4 =$

2. Explain your estimation strategy for Question 1B.

Before starting this assessment activity, decide if students will complete the problems in groups or individually. One suggestion is to have students work on *Questions 1–3* as a group. This will allow students an opportunity to share their strategies and the patterns they see. Students can then answer *Questions 4–7* independently. These last four questions ask students to use the patterns they have found to answer questions about other Many-Eyed Dragonflies.

Another option is to have students answer all but *Questions 6–7* with their groups.

Introduce students to planet Gzorp using the introductory vignette on *The Many-Eyed Dragonfly* Assessment Blackline Masters. Explain to students that they are going to help Professor Peabody study the growth pattern of the Many-Eyed Dragonfly. Tell them you will evaluate their work using the Student Rubrics: *Telling, Solving,* and *Knowing.* Review each rubric using either rubric posters or transparencies of the rubrics. As part of this review, ask the following questions:

What strategies can you use to solve problems about the Many-Eyed Dragonfly? Students may suggest:

• Creating a data table.

• Recognizing patterns and generalizing the patterns to solve problems.

• Using a calculator.

• Modeling the growth pattern using square-inch tiles.

• Drawing pictures.

• Using number sentences.

When writing about your solution, what information should you include? Students may suggest:

• Include words to explain how you found your solution.

• Include pictures, tables, or number sentences to support or illustrate your solution.

• Include a description of any patterns you used to find your solution.

• Include a justification of your strategies. How do you know they work all the time?

Reviewing the rubrics before beginning the problem will help students know the expectations. Students can refer to the rubrics in their *Student Guides* as they work. Once this discussion is complete, students should complete the problems on *The Many-Eyed Dragonfly* Assessment Blackline Masters.

A Age in Years	N Number of Eye Squares
1	1
2	5
3	9
4	13
5	17
6	21

Figure 9: *The growth of a Many-Eyed Dragonfly*

Remind students that they can use any tools in the mathematics classroom such as calculators and square-inch tiles.

Question 1 asks students to draw a four-year-old Many-Eyed Dragonfly and then asks how many eyes it has. In *Question 2,* students create a data table for Professor Peabody as shown in Figure 9. If students have difficulty with this question, help them identify the two variables they are comparing: the age of the Many-Eyed Dragonfly and the total number of eye squares. Suggest that students begin their data tables with the information they already know; that is, the number of squares for a 1-, 2-, 3-, and 4-year-old Many-Eyed Dragonfly. They can then begin extending the chart. In *Question 3,* students are asked to describe any patterns they see. The following are examples of patterns students have described:

- After the first year, you add four eye squares each year.

- The total number of eye squares is always an odd number.

- If you multiply the age of the Many-Eyed Dragonfly by 4 and then subtract 3, you have the total number of eye squares for that Many-Eyed Dragonfly.

- If you subtract 1 from the age of the Many-Eyed Dragonfly, multiply that number by 4, and then add 1, you will have the total number of eye squares for that Many-Eyed Dragonfly.

In *Question 4,* students are asked to find the number of eye squares a 12-year-old Many-Eyed Dragonfly has. Students can find this information by extending the data table, drawing a picture, or using square-inch tiles to build the Many-Eyed Dragonfly.

Question 5 asks students to find out how many eye squares a 50-year-old Many-Eyed Dragonfly has. This question can be solved using many different strategies. A student may choose to:

- Draw a picture of a 50-year-old Many-Eyed Dragonfly.

- Use a calculator to continually add 4 eye squares for each year of the Many-Eyed Dragonfly's age from 2 years old to 50 years old. Students need to remember that when the Many-Eyed Dragonfly is one year old, it has only 1 eye square. This 1 eye square must be added in at some point.

- Extend the data table to include a 50-year-old Many-Eyed Dragonfly.

- Use the number sentence $50 \times 4 - 3$ to find the total number of eye squares. This number sentence works because the Many-Eyed Dragonfly has 4 legs, each leg has 50 squares (one for each year), except the middle tile is part of each of the 4 legs and so is counted four times. You only need to count it one time, so you have to subtract the three extra times.

- Use the number sentence $(50 - 1) \times 4 + 1$ to find the total number of eye squares. This number sentence works because each leg has $(50 - 1)$ or 49 squares in each leg, not including the center square. There are 4 legs on each Dragonfly. After multiplying 49×4, you must add the center square into the total. Although students are often unable to write this number sentence in symbols, they can describe this strategy in words and give examples.

While several strategies are listed, the first three are not very efficient. If a group or an individual is using one of these strategies, suggest that they look back at their data table and try to find a relationship between the age and the total number of eye squares. If a group or an individual needs this extra support, be sure to make a note to consider it when scoring the final work.

Students must show how they found their solutions. They should also use words to explain their strategies.

Students are asked to explain a strategy for finding the number of eye squares for a Many-Eyed Dragonfly of any age in *Question 6.* After students complete *Question 6,* give them an opportunity to revise their work based on your input. Score the completed work using the *TIMS Multidimensional Rubric.* You can now compare this problem to other open-response assessment problems completed earlier this year.

In *Question 7,* students will need to work backwards to estimate the age of the Many-Eyed Dragonfly. For example, if students recognize that there are four eye squares for each year of growth and that 1001 is close to 1000, they can divide 1000 by four to estimate the age of 250 years.

Journal Prompt

Evaluate how well your group worked together. What strategies did you use in your group to help each member understand the problem?

TIMS Tip

You can score *The Many-Eyed Dragonfly* using all three dimensions of the rubric. One suggestion is to score *Questions 1–5* and *7* using the Solving and Knowing dimensions of the *TIMS Multidimensional Rubric.* Then score *Question 6* using the Telling dimension of the rubric.

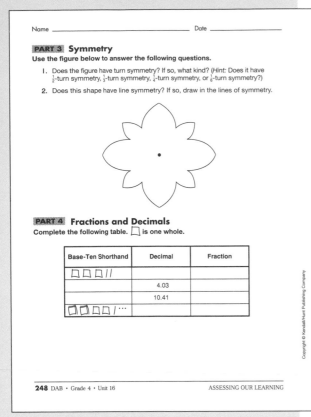

Discovery Assignment Book - page 248 (Answers on p. 82)

Math Facts

DPP Bit I provides practice with math facts.

Homework and Practice

- DPP Challenge J asks students to compare and order metric measurements. DPP items K and L provide computation practice.

- Assign Parts 3 and 4 of the Home Practice.

Answers for Parts 3 and 4 of the Home Practice are in the Answer Key at the end of this lesson and at the end of this unit.

Assessment

To help you score students' work, some questions specific to this task are listed below:

Solving

- Did students identify all the elements of the problem and their relationship to one another? For example, did they recognize that you add four eye squares for each year of growth after the first year? Did they recognize the relationship between the age of the Many-Eyed Dragonfly and the total number of eye squares?

- Did students use problem-solving strategies efficiently? Did they use the tools available to them such as data tables, calculators, or square-inch tiles? Did they organize their work?

- Did students relate this problem to previously learned mathematics? For example, did they use what they learned about functions in Unit 15 to help them see patterns? Did students look for ways to use operations to help them define the growth pattern?

- Did students persist in the problem-solving process until a solution was reached? Did they continue to work to verify their solution, possibly finding alternative solutions?

- Did students look back to see if their solutions were reasonable, based on their data? For example, if they reported that all Many-Eyed Dragonflies have an odd number of squares, did they verify that their answers for the number of squares are odd?

Knowing

- Did students use appropriate mathematical operations for completing this task? For example, did they discover ways to represent the growth pattern using number sentences?

- Did students use pictures or data tables to help answer questions? Were students able to translate the patterns in the data table into number sentences or describe them using words?

- If students used classroom tools, were they used correctly? For example, did they use their calculators and square-inch tiles correctly?

- Did students use their math facts correctly? Were their computations correct?

Telling

- Were students' explanations of their problem-solving strategies complete? Did they include general plans or formulas for finding the number of squares in any Many-Eyed Dragonfly? Did they describe their problem-solving process?

- Were their written responses clear and detailed? Were there gaps in the explanations? Did they give examples to clarify their explanations?

- Did students include supporting arguments for their solutions? For example, did they refer to patterns they saw in the data table? Did they look for more than one solution to justify their answers?

- Did students use pictures or data tables to help explain their work? For example, did they extend their data tables from *Question 2* as a way to support plans or formulas?

- Did they use correct number sentences?

Two samples of student work scored on all three dimensions of the *TIMS Multidimensional Rubric* are shown in the next four pages.

Written work from Student A:

1. A. Draw a 4-year-old Many-Eyed Dragonfly.

B. How many eyes does it have? 13

2. Professor Peabody was asked to study the Many-Eyed Dragonfly. He wants to organize his data using a table. Set up a data table for Professor Peabody. Think about the two variables that the Professor is going to study. Extend the data table until you can see a pattern.

N Years or age	C No. eyes
1 Year	1 eye
2 Years	5 eyes
3 Years	9 eyes
4 years	13 eyes
5 yeas	17 eyes
6 Years	21 eyes
7 Years	25 eyes
8 Year	29 eyes
9 Year	33 eyes
10 Years	37 eyes
11 Years	41 eyes
12 Yeas	45 eyes
13 Years	49 eyes
14	53 eyes
15	57 eyes

3. What patterns do you see in the data table? They all are odd Numbers or they added four to all the Numbers

4. A. How many eye squares does a 12-year-old Many-Eyed Dragonfly have?

45 eyes

B. Show how you solved this problem, explaining your strategy. after we found the pattern we added four to the frist answer we got. The Pattern we anwer they add four to every anwer or all of the numbers the numbers are odd.

5. A. How many eye squares does a 50-year-old Many-Eyed Dragonfly have?

197 eyes

B. Show how you solved this problem, explaining your strategy.

49 × 4 = 196 + 7 = 197 eyes

6. Write a paragraph explaining how to find the number of eye squares for any age Many-Eyed Dragonfly. Tell how you discovered your strategy and how you know it works. You may need to write on the back of this paper.

only Professor peabody numbers. had to think of odd last number. add 4 to the number number. Or if the is 60 he only the do this → 59 × 4 + 1 = 237. had to

7. A. Estimate the age of a Many-Eyed Dragonfly that has 1001 eye squares.

250 Years.

B. Show how you solved this problem, explaining your strategy.

250 × 4 + 1 = 1001

On the Solving dimension, Student A received a score of 4. She recognized the relationship between the age and number of squares in a Many-Eyed Dragonfly. She organized her work in a table and looked for ways to represent the patterns in the table using number sentences. She persisted in the process until a solution was reached, verified her solution using patterns identified in the table, made connections, and drew appropriate conclusions. For example, in her response to *Question 4* she tells us that, "all of the numbers are odd" and in *Question 6,* "Professor Peabody only has to think of odd numbers."

On the Knowing dimension, Student A also received a 4. Her correct responses and explanations show that she understands the concepts. She translated the situation in the problem into pictures, data tables,

number sentences, and words. Her answers are correct, although there are minor errors in her number sentence for *Question 5.* The correct number sentence should read: $49 \times 4 + 1 = 196 + 1 = 197$ eyes.

On the Telling dimension, Student A is at level 3. Although her responses are correct and the reader can interpret her strategy, her written descriptions are unclear. For example, to find the number of squares for any age Many-Eyed Dragonfly, she tells us to "add 4 to the last number." She illustrates her strategy, however, with a number sentence for a different strategy: "if the number is 60 he only has to do this: $59 \times 4 + 1 = 237$." She does not explain how she got from the first strategy to the second or why the second strategy works.

Solving	Level 4	Level 3	Level 2	Level 1
Identifies the elements of the problem and their relationships to one another	All major elements identified	Most elements identified	Some, but shows little understanding of relationships	Few or none
Uses problem-solving strategies which are…	Systematic, complete, efficient, and possibly elegant	Systematic and nearly complete, but not efficient	Incomplete or unsystematic	Not evident or inappropriate
Organizes relevant information…	Systematically and efficiently	Systematically, with minor errors	Unsystematically	Not at all
Relates the problem and solution to previously encountered mathematics and makes connections that are…	At length, elegant, and meaningful	Evident	Brief or logically unsound	Not evident
Persists in the problem-solving process…	At length	Until a solution is reached	Briefly	Not at all
Looks back to examine the reasonableness of the solution and draws conclusions that are…	Insightful and comprehensive	Correct	Incorrect or logically unsound	Not present

Knowing	Level 4	Level 3	Level 2	Level 1
Understands the task's mathematical concepts, their properties and applications…	Completely	Nearly completely	Partially	Not at all
Translates between words, pictures, symbols, tables, graphs, and real situations…	Readily and without errors	With minor errors	With major errors	Not at all
Uses tools (measuring devices, graphs, tables, calculators, etc.) and procedures…	Correctly and efficiently	Correctly or with minor errors	Incorrectly	Not at all
Uses knowledge of the facts of mathematics (geometry definitions, math facts, etc.)…	Correctly	With minor errors	With major errors	Not at all

Telling	Level 4	Level 3	Level 2	Level 1
Includes response with an explanation and/or description which is…	Complete and clear	Fairly complete and clear	Perhaps ambiguous or unclear	Totally unclear or irrelevant
Presents supporting arguments which are…	Strong and sound	Logically sound, but may contain minor gaps	Incomplete or logically unsound	Not present
Uses pictures, symbols, tables, and graphs which are…	Correct and clearly relevant	Present with minor errors or somewhat irrelevant	Present with errors and/or irrelevant	Not present or completely inappropriate
Uses terminology…	Clearly and precisely	With minor errors	With major errors	Not at all

Figure 10: *Student A's work scored using the three dimensions of the* TIMS Multidimensional Rubric

Written work from Student B:

1. A. Draw a 4-year-old Many-Eyed Dragonfly.

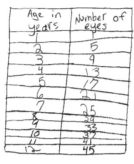

   B. How many eyes does it have? 13 eyes

2. Professor Peabody was asked to study the Many-Eyed Dragonfly. He wants to organize his data using a table. Set up a data table for Professor Peabody. Think about the two variables that the Professor is going to study. Extend the data table until you can see a pattern.

Age in years	Number of eyes
1	1
2	5
3	9
4	13
5	17
6	21
7	25
8	29
9	33
10	37
11	41
12	45

3. What patterns do you see in the data table? The number of eyes is always odd, also the number of eyes go up 4 each time. The last didget of the number of eyes go in the same pattern: 1, 5, 9, 3, 7.

4. A. How many eye squares does a 12-year-old Many-Eyed Dragonfly have? It has 45 eye squares.

   B. Show how you solved this problem, explaining your strategy. I looked at my data table.

5. A. How many eye squares does a 50-year-old Many-Eyed Dragonfly have? It would have 201 eye squares.

   B. Show how you solved this problem, explaining your strategy. We did the problem by 50x4-3=197, thats how we found the answer

6. Write a paragraph explaining how to find the number of eye squares for any age Many-Eyed Dragonfly. Tell how you discovered your strategy and how you know it works. You may need to write on the back of this paper.

   You can find out how many eye squares there are by timesing the age by 4 then subtract 3. You do that because then if you don't subtract 3 then you will come up with an answer 3 numbers above. So then you will have to subtract 3 and you will come up with the right answer.

7. A. Estimate the age of a Many-Eyed Dragonfly that has 1001 eye squares. A 251, year old Many Eyed-Octupi.

   B. Show how you solved this problem, explaining your strategy. We solved it by useing 251 x 4-3=1001.

Student B received a score of 3 on the Solving dimension. He organized his information correctly in a data table and used it to answer the questions and derive a strategy. However, he did not persist in the process at length or check his solutions. For example, his answer to **Question 5A** is 201 eye squares, but when he showed how to use the number sentence to find the answer in **Question 5B,** his answer is 197. Although he found an answer to **Question 7,** he could have used a more efficient strategy to find an estimate instead of an exact answer.

On the Knowing dimension he received a 3. His explanations show that he understood the task although he did not reconcile the two different answers he gave in

Question 5. He translated the information into a picture, a data table, and number sentences, with only minor errors.

He also received a 3 on the Telling dimension. His explanations are clear and his number sentences are correct. There are no gaps in his description of an interesting pattern in the data table, "The last digit of the number of eyes go in the same pattern: 1, 5, 9, 3, 7." However, his response to **Question 6** has minor gaps in his paragraph describing the process for finding the number of squares. He offers a rationale for his number sentence, but does not explain why subtracting 3 gives the correct answer each time.

Solving	Level 4	Level 3	Level 2	Level 1
Identifies the elements of the problem and their relationships to one another	All major elements identified ✗	Most elements identified	Some, but shows little understanding of relationships	Few or none
Uses problem-solving strategies which are…	Systematic, complete, efficient, and possibly elegant	Systematic and nearly complete, but not efficient	Incomplete or unsystematic	Not evident or inappropriate
Organizes relevant information…	Systematically and efficiently	Systematically, with minor errors ✗	Unsystematically	Not at all
Relates the problem and solution to previously encountered mathematics and makes connections that are…	At length, elegant, and meaningful	Evident ✗	Brief or logically unsound	Not evident
Persists in the problem-solving process…	At length	Until a solution is reached ✗	Briefly	Not at all
Looks back to examine the reasonableness of the solution and draws conclusions that are…	Insightful and comprehensive	Correct	Incorrect or ✗ logically unsound	Not present

Knowing	Level 4	Level 3	Level 2	Level 1
Understands the task's mathematical concepts, their properties and applications…	Completely	✗ Nearly completely	Partially	Not at all
Translates between words, pictures, symbols, tables, graphs, and real situations…	Readily and without errors	With minor errors ✗	With major errors	Not at all
Uses tools (measuring devices, graphs, tables, calculators, etc.) and procedures…	Correctly and efficiently	Correctly or with minor errors ✗	Incorrectly	Not at all
Uses knowledge of the facts of mathematics (geometry definitions, math facts, etc.)…	Correctly ✗	With minor errors	With major errors	Not at all

Telling	Level 4	Level 3	Level 2	Level 1
Includes response with an explanation and/or description which is…	Complete and clear	Fairly complete and clear ✗	Perhaps ambiguous or unclear	Totally unclear or irrelevant
Presents supporting arguments which are…	Strong and sound	Logically sound, but may contain minor gaps ✗	Incomplete or logically unsound	Not present
Uses pictures, symbols, tables, and graphs which are…	Correct and clearly relevant	Present with minor errors or somewhat irrelevant ✗	Present with errors and/or irrelevant	Not present or completely inappropriate
Uses terminology…	Clearly and precisely	✗ With minor errors	With major errors	Not at all

Figure 11: *Student B's work scored using the three dimensions of the* TIMS Multidimensional Rubric

At a Glance

Math Facts and Daily Practice and Problems

DPP Bit I provides practice with math facts. Challenge J reviews metric measurement. Items K and L are computation practice.

Teaching the Activity

1. Decide which parts of *The Many-Eyed Dragonfly* Assessment Blackline Masters will be completed in small groups and which parts will be completed independently.
2. Remind students of their work with creatures from planet Gzorp in Unit 15 (optional).
3. Introduce the Many-Eyed Dragonfly to students, explaining that they will explore the growth patterns of these creatures.
4. Discuss problem-solving strategies they can use to solve this problem.
5. Allow time for students to answer each question and to write about their solutions.
6. Allow students to revise their written work after your input.
7. Score student work. Compare this work to other work on similar problems.
8. Add this problem to students' collection folders.

Homework

Assign Parts 3 and 4 of the Home Practice.

Assessment

Use the Solving, Knowing, and Telling dimensions of the *TIMS Multidimensional Rubric* to assess student work on *The Many-Eyed Dragonfly* Assessment Blackline Masters.

Answer Key is on pages 82–84.

Notes:

Name _____   Date _____

The Many-Eyed Dragonfly

Far, far, away there is a planet called Gzorp. The creatures on this planet are made up of squares. Each year, they grow by adding more squares. Each creature has a rule as to how it can grow. Professor Peabody has been sent to study the creatures on this planet.

One of the creatures he has found to study is a Many-Eyed Dragonfly.

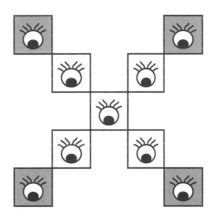

A Many-Eyed Dragonfly has only one eye square when it is 1 year old. A 1-year-old, a 2-year-old, and a 3-year-old Many-Eyed Dragonfly are shown below. Many-Eyed Dragonflies follow the same growth pattern each year.

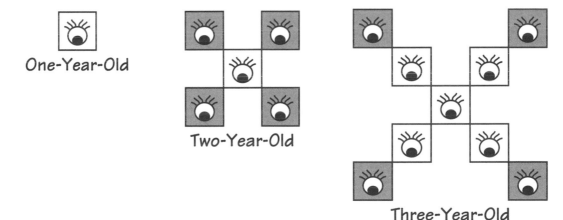

One-Year-Old

Two-Year-Old

Three-Year-Old

1. **A.** Draw a 4-year-old Many-Eyed Dragonfly.

    B. How many eyes does it have?

2. Professor Peabody was asked to study the Many-Eyed Dragonfly. He wants to organize his data using a table. Set up a data table for Professor Peabody. Think about the two variables the Professor is going to study. Extend the data table until you can see a pattern.

3. What patterns do you see in the data table?

4. A. How many eye squares does a 12-year-old Many-Eyed Dragonfly have?

B. Show how you solved this problem, explaining your strategy.

5. A. How many eye squares does a 50-year-old Many-Eyed Dragonfly have?

B. Show how you solved this problem, explaining your strategy.

6. Write a paragraph explaining how to find the number of eye squares for a Many-Eyed Dragonfly of any age. Tell how you discovered your strategy and how you know it works. You may need to write on the back of this paper.

7. **A.** Estimate the age of a Many-Eyed Dragonfly that has 1001 eye squares.

   B. Show how you solved this problem, explaining your strategy.

Name _____ Date _____

_____

Two-column Data Table, Blackline Master

Discovery Assignment Book - page 248

Discovery Assignment Book (p. 248)

Home Practice*

Part 3. Symmetry

1. Yes, $\frac{1}{4}$-turn symmetry

2. Yes.

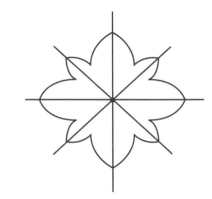

Part 4. Fractions and Decimals

Base-Ten Shorthand	Decimal	Fraction
☐☐☐ //	3.2	$3\frac{2}{10}$ or $3\frac{1}{5}$
☐☐☐☐ ···	4.03	$4\frac{3}{100}$
☐ //// ·	10.41	$10\frac{41}{100}$
☐☐☐☐ / ···	22.13	$22\frac{13}{100}$

*Answers for all the Home Practice in the *Discovery Assignment Book* are at the end of the unit.

82   URG • Grade 4 • Unit 16 • Lesson 4 • Answer Key

Unit Resource Guide (pp. 78–79)

1. A.

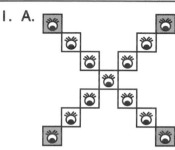

B. 13 eyes

2. Length of students' tables will vary.

A Age in Years	N Number of Eye Squares
1	1
2	5
3	9
4	13
5	17
6	21

3. Possible patterns: The number of eyes increases by 4 for each year; the number of eye squares is always odd; the last digit in the number of eyes follows a repeating pattern (1, 5, 9, 3, 7); the total number of eye squares equals four times the age less 3; and the total number of eye squares for any dragonfly can be found by multiplying the age of a dragonfly that is a year younger by four and then adding 1: $N = (A - 1) \times 4 + 1$ where N = number of eyes and A = age in years.*

4. A. 45 eye squares

B. Possible strategies include continuing the data table, making a many-eyed dragonfly with square-inch tiles, drawing a picture, or following a pattern described in the answer to *Question 3.**

5. A. 197 eye squares

B. Answers will vary. One possible strategy: $50 \times 4 - 3 = 197$.*

Name _____ Date _____

1. **A.** Draw a 4-year-old Many-Eyed Dragonfly.

   B. How many eyes does it have?

2. Professor Peabody was asked to study the Many-Eyed Dragonfly. He wants to organize his data using a table. Set up a data table for Professor Peabody. Think about the two variables the Professor is going to study. Extend the data table until you can see a pattern.

Assessment Blackline Master

Unit Resource Guide - page 78

Name _____ Date _____

3. What patterns do you see in the data table?

4. **A.** How many eye squares does a 12-year-old Many-Eyed Dragonfly have?

   B. Show how you solved this problem, explaining your strategy.

5. **A.** How many eye squares does a 50-year-old Many-Eyed Dragonfly have?

   B. Show how you solved this problem, explaining your strategy.

Assessment Blackline Master

Unit Resource Guide - page 79

*Answers and/or discussion are included in the Lesson Guide.

Name _____ Date _____

6. Write a paragraph explaining how to find the number of eye squares for a Many-Eyed Dragonfly of any age. Tell how you discovered your strategy and how you know it works. You may need to write on the back of this paper.

7. **A.** Estimate the age of a Many-Eyed Dragonfly that has 1001 eye squares.

    B. Show how you solved this problem, explaining your strategy.

Assessment Blackline Master

Unit Resource Guide - page 80

Unit Resource Guide (p. 80)

6. Answers will vary. See two sample student paragraphs, Student A and Student B, in Lesson Guide 4.*

7. **A.** About 250 years*

    B. Answers will vary.

*Answers and/or discussion are included in the Lesson Guide.

Lesson
5

End-of-Year Test

Estimated Class Sessions
2

Lesson Overview

Students take a year-end paper-and-pencil test. This is a short-item test that assesses concepts and skills learned throughout this school year.

Key Content

• Assessing skills and concepts learned this year.

Math Facts

DPP Bit O provides practice computing with multiples of 10 and Task P reviews multiplication and division with zeros and ones.

Homework

1. Assign Parts 5 and 6 of the Home Practice either in this lesson or in Lesson 6.
2. Students study for the *Division Facts Inventory Test* using *Triangle Flash Cards*.

Curriculum Sequence

Before This Unit

In Unit 5 Lesson 8, Unit 8 Lesson 6, and Unit 12 Lesson 9 students took tests similar to the *End-of-Year Test*.

Materials List

Supplies and Copies

Student	Teacher
Supplies for Each Student • calculator • ruler • pattern blocks • base-ten pieces	**Supplies**
Copies • 1 copy of *End-of-Year Test* per student (*Unit Resource Guide* Pages 90–92)	**Copies/Transparencies**

All blackline masters including assessment, transparency, and DPP masters are also on the Teacher Resource CD.

Daily Practice and Problems and Home Practice

DPP items M–P (*Unit Resource Guide* Pages 19–20)
Home Practice Parts 5–6 (*Discovery Assignment Book* Page 249)

Note: Classrooms whose pacing differs significantly from the suggested pacing of the units should use the Math Facts Calendar in Section 4 of the *Facts Resource Guide* to ensure students receive the complete math facts program.

Suggestions for using the DPPs are on page 88.

M. Bit: Time (URG p. 19) 🕐

1. John ate dinner 2 hours and 15 minutes after he got home from school. If he ate dinner at 5:20, what time did he get home from school?

2. Shannon took her little cousin to the park. They left the house at 4:15. It took them 20 minutes to walk to the park. They played for 45 minutes and then walked back home. What time did they arrive home?

O. Bit: Multiplying with Zeros (URG p. 20)

The n in each number sentence stands for a missing number. Find the number that makes each sentence true.

A. $80 \times n = 320$
B. $n \times 30 = 27{,}000$
C. $8000 \times n = 56{,}000$
D. $50 \times n = 10{,}000$
E. $400 \times n = 40{,}000$
F. $300 \times n = 1500$

N. Task: Pattern Block Fractions (URG p. 19)

If the shape below is one whole, name the fraction each shape in A–D represents.

A.

B.

C.

D.

P. Task: Zeros and Ones (URG p. 20)

1. A. $8 \times 1 =$ B. $4 \div 0 =$
   C. $0 \div 9 =$ D. $1 \div 1 =$
   E. $12 \div 1 =$ F. $5 \div 0 =$
   G. $7 \times 0 =$ H. $3 \div 3 =$

2. Justify your reasoning for Questions 1B and 1C using a related multiplication sentence.

Teaching the Activity

Students take the *End-of-Year Test* independently. It is designed to take one class period; however, make adjustments if more time is needed. The first part of this test assesses competency with the use of paper-and-pencil methods and mental math strategies for computation and estimation. This part of the test is to be completed without a calculator. After students complete Part 1 they may begin Part 2. Students should have a calculator, ruler, pattern blocks, and base-ten pieces available for their use. Students read and follow the directions for each item. If all units were not completed, choose the items appropriate for your class.

Math Facts

DPP Bit O provides practice with math facts using unknowns in number sentences with multiples of 10. DPP Task P reviews multiplication and division with zeros and ones.

Homework and Practice

- DPP Bit M provides word problems that involve elapsed time. Task N provides practice naming a fractional part of a whole.
- Remind students to use the *Triangle Flash Cards* to study the division facts.
- Assign Parts 5 and 6 of the Home Practice in the *Discovery Assignment Book* here or in Lesson 6.

Answers for Parts 5 and 6 of the Home Practice are in the Answer Key at the end of this lesson and at the end of this unit.

Assessment

The *End-of-Year Test* assesses skills and concepts studied this year.

Name _____ Date _____

PART 5 School Days
Use the data below to answer the following questions.

Country	Average Number of School Days
U.S.A.	180
Canada	186
England	192
Japan	243

1. About how many days will a child in England have gone to school when he or she has attended school for 5 years?

2. Yoshi lives in Japan. He has gone to school for 5 years. Jackie lives in the United States. She has gone to school for 5 years. About how many more days has Yoshi gone to school than Jackie?

3. About how many days does a student in the U.S.A. have to go to school to graduate from high school? (To graduate from high school, most students must go to school for 13 years including kindergarten.)

PART 6 Multiplication and Division Practice
Solve the following problems using paper and pencil or mental math. Show your work on a separate sheet of paper. Estimate to make sure your answers are reasonable. Explain your estimation strategy for D.

A. $64 \times 77 =$ _____   B. $23 \times 48 =$ _____

C. $70 \times 56 =$ _____   D. $3540 \times 4 =$ _____

E. $875 \div 7 =$ _____   F. $5960 \div 6 =$ _____

G. $3000 \div 50 =$ _____   H. $7812 \div 9 =$ _____

ASSESSING OUR LEARNING   DAB • Grade 4 • Unit 16 **249**

Discovery Assignment Book - page 249 *(Answers on p. 93)*

Estimated Class Sessions

2

At a Glance

Math Facts and Daily Practice and Problems

DPP Bit M provides practice with elapsed time. Task N provides practice with fractions. DPP Bit O provides practice computing with multiples of 10 and Task P reviews multiplication and division with zeros and ones.

Teaching the Activity

1. Students complete Part 1 of the *End-of-Year Test* without a calculator.
2. Students complete Part 2 of the test using the tools they used in mathematics class throughout the year.

Homework

1. Assign Parts 5 and 6 of the Home Practice either in this lesson or in Lesson 6.
2. Students study for the *Division Facts Inventory Test* using *Triangle Flash Cards*.

Answer Key is on pages 93–94.

Notes:

End-of-Year Test

Part 1

For this part of the test, use only paper and pencil or mental math to solve the problems. Estimate to make sure your answers are reasonable.

1. 1225
    − 397

2. 1362
    + 3758

3. 2003
    − 795

4. 13
    × 28

5. 5842
    × 4

6. 97
    × 50

7. 3)88

8. 5)735

9. **A.** Explain your estimation strategy for Question 6.

    B. Explain a mental math strategy for Question 3.

10. Bessie Coleman School is collecting paper for a recycling program. In January, they collected 1512 pounds of paper; in February, they collected 1073 pounds of paper; and, in March, they collected 1396 pounds of paper. Estimate the amount of paper collected over this three-month period. Write a number sentence to show how you found your estimate.

11. Estimate the measure (in degrees) of each of the following angles.

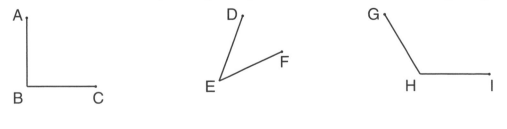

_____   _____   _____

Copyright © Kendall/Hunt Publishing Company

Part 2

Use what you have learned in mathematics class this year to solve the following problems. You may use any tool you usually use in class including a calculator.

12. Complete the following table. A flat ⌂ is equal to 1.

Base-Ten Shorthand	Decimal	Fraction
⌂ ⌂ // ·····		$2\frac{25}{100}$
	1.6	
		$3\frac{4}{100}$
⌂ ⌂ /// :····		

13. Construct a quadrilateral ABCD using the following rules:
    A. $\overleftrightarrow{AB}$ must be parallel to $\overleftrightarrow{DC}$.
    B. $\overleftrightarrow{AD}$ must be perpendicular to $\overleftrightarrow{DC}$.
    C. The measure of Angle A equals 90 degrees.
    D. The measure of Angle B is less than 90 degrees.

14. Put the following fractions in order from smallest to largest.

    A. $\frac{1}{6}, \frac{1}{4}, \frac{1}{2}, \frac{1}{3}$

    B. $\frac{4}{12}, \frac{1}{12}, \frac{13}{12}, \frac{14}{12}$

15. If a yellow hexagon is equal to 1 whole, name the following numbers each figure represents. You may use pattern blocks to help you.

A.

B.

16. Use the graph below to answer the following questions. Use a separate sheet of paper to record your answers.

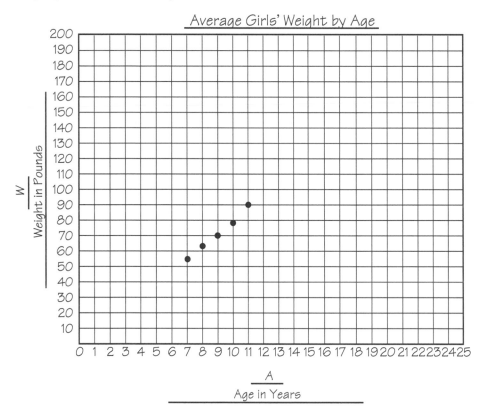

A. Describe the graph.

B. Do the points lie close to a straight line? If so, use a ruler to draw a best-fit line.

C. If possible, predict the weight of an average 14-year-old girl. Explain your answer.

D. If possible, predict the weight of an average 23-year-old woman. Explain your answer.

E. If possible, predict the weight of an average 1-year-old girl. Explain your answer.

Discovery Assignment Book (p. 249)

Home Practice*

Part 5. School Days

Answers will vary. One possible solution is given for each question.

1. $200 \times 5 = 1000$ days

2. $250 - 180 = 70; 70 \times 5 = 350$ days

3. $200 \times 13 = 2600$ days

Part 6. Multiplication and Division Practice

A. 4928	**B.** 1104
C. 3920	**D.** 14,160
E. 125	**F.** 993 R2
G. 60	**H.** 868

Possible strategy for D: 3500×4 is 3500 doubled or 7000 and 7000 doubled again or 14,000.

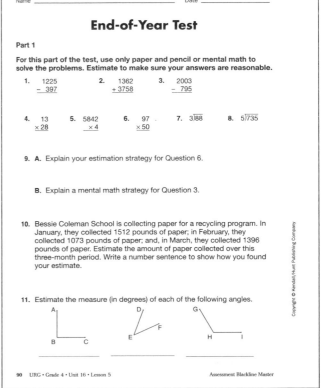

Discovery Assignment Book - page 249

Unit Resource Guide (p. 90)

End-of-Year Test

1. 828
2. 5120
3. 1208
4. 364
5. 23,368
6. 4850
7. 29 R1
8. 147
9. **A.** Possible strategy: $100 \times 50 = 5000$

   B. Possible strategy: Count up 5 to 800, 1200 to 2000, and 3 more to 2003; $5 + 1200 + 3 = 1208$.

10. Answers will vary. One possible estimate: $1500 + 1100 + 1400 = 4000$ pounds

11. Estimates will vary. 90°, 45°, 120°; accept answers within 10° larger or smaller.

Unit Resource Guide - page 90

*Answers for all the Home Practice in the *Discovery Assignment Book* are at the end of the unit.

Name _____ Date _____

Part 2

Use what you have learned in mathematics class this year to solve the following problems. You may use any tool you usually use in class including a calculator.

12. Complete the following table. A flat ☐ is equal to 1.

Base-Ten Shorthand	Decimal	Fraction
☐☐// ⁚⁚⁚⁚		$2\frac{25}{100}$
	1.6	
		$3\frac{4}{100}$
◻☐///:⁚⁚⁚		

13. Construct a quadrilateral ABCD using the following rules:
A. $\overline{AB}$ must be parallel to $\overline{DC}$.
B. $\overline{AD}$ must be perpendicular to $\overline{DC}$.
C. The measure of Angle A equals 90 degrees.
D. The measure of Angle B is less than 90 degrees.

14. Put the following fractions in order from smallest to largest.
A. $\frac{1}{6}, \frac{1}{4}, \frac{1}{2}, \frac{1}{3}$

B. $\frac{4}{12}, \frac{1}{12}, \frac{13}{12}, \frac{14}{12}$

Unit Resource Guide - page 91

Name _____ Date _____

15. If a yellow hexagon is equal to 1 whole, name the following numbers each figure represents. You may use pattern blocks to help you.

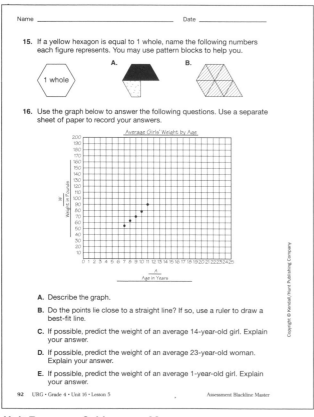

16. Use the graph below to answer the following questions. Use a separate sheet of paper to record your answers.

A. Describe the graph.

B. Do the points lie close to a straight line? If so, use a ruler to draw a best-fit line.

C. If possible, predict the weight of an average 14-year-old girl. Explain your answer.

D. If possible, predict the weight of an average 23-year-old woman. Explain your answer.

E. If possible, predict the weight of an average 1-year-old girl. Explain your answer.

Unit Resource Guide - page 92

Unit Resource Guide (pp. 91–92)

12.

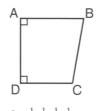

Base-Ten Shorthand	Decimal	Fraction
☐☐// ⁚⁚⁚⁚	2.25	$2\frac{25}{100}$
☐//////	1.6	$1\frac{6}{10}$
☐☐☐ ⁚⁚⁚⁚	3.04	$3\frac{4}{100}$
◻☐///:⁚⁚⁚	11.36	$11\frac{36}{100}$

13. One possible solution:

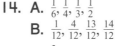

14. A. $\frac{1}{6}, \frac{1}{4}, \frac{1}{3}, \frac{1}{2}$
B. $\frac{1}{12}, \frac{4}{12}, \frac{13}{12}, \frac{14}{12}$

15. A. $\frac{3}{4}$

B. $\frac{7}{6}$ or $1\frac{1}{6}$

16. A.–B.

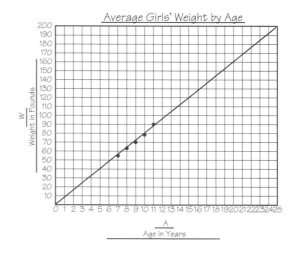

C. Between 100 and 120 pounds (Estimates will vary.)

D. According to the graph, an average 23-year-old weighs between 180–190 pounds. Although a 23-year-old could weigh 180–190 pounds, this value is high for the average weight of a 23-year-old. Students should see that extrapolating this far beyond the last data point is unreliable.

E. According to the graph, an average 1-year-old weighs about 10 pounds. Students should see that extrapolating this far beyond the first data point is unreliable.

Portfolios

Lesson Overview

Estimated Class Sessions

1-2

Students review the work they collected in their portfolios during this school year. They look for examples that show what they know, how they solve problems, and how they communicate their problem-solving strategies to others. Students look for work that demonstrates their growth in mathematics over the school year.

Key Content

- Reflecting on one's own work.
- Organizing work in a portfolio.
- Assessing fluency with the division facts.

Math Facts

DPP Task R is an assessment of all the division facts.

Homework

Students share their portfolios with their parents for homework.

Assessment

1. DPP Task R is the *Division Facts Inventory Test* and assesses fluency with the division facts. Record students' fluency with the division facts on the *Observational Assessment Record*.
2. Transfer appropriate Unit 16 observations to the *Individual Assessment Record Sheets*.

Materials List

Supplies and Copies

Student	Teacher
Supplies for Each Student • portfolio folder from Unit 2 • collection folder from Unit 2 • two different-colored pencils or a pen and pencil	**Supplies**
Copies • 1 copy of *Division Facts Inventory Test* per student (*Unit Resource Guide* Page 22)	**Copies/Transparencies**

All blackline masters including assessment, transparency, and DPP masters are also on the Teacher Resource CD.

Student Books
Portfolios (*Student Guide* Page 439)

Daily Practice and Problems and Home Practice
DPP items Q–R (*Unit Resource Guide* Pages 20–21)

Note: Classrooms whose pacing differs significantly from the suggested pacing of the units should use the Math Facts Calendar in Section 4 of the *Facts Resource Guide* to ensure students receive the complete math facts program.

Assessment Tools
Observational Assessment Record (*Unit Resource Guide* Pages 9–10)
Individual Assessment Record Sheet (*Teacher Implementation Guide,* Assessment section)

Q. Bit: United States Population (URG p. 20) 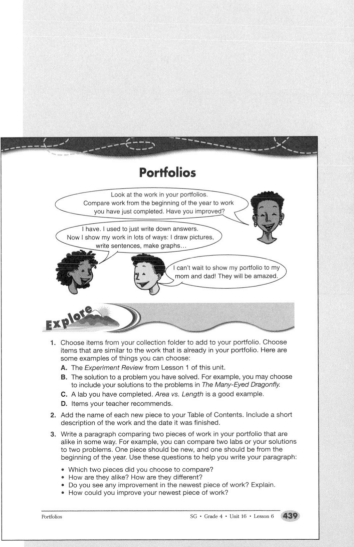 [N]

In 1790 the first U.S. census was taken. There were 3,929,200 people in the United States. By 2000 there were 281,421,906 people in the United States.

1. About how many more people were there in 2000 as compared to 1790?
2. This change in population occurred over how many years?

R. Task: Division Facts Inventory Test (URG p. 21) [5/7]

Have two pens or pencils of different colors ready. During the first four minutes of the test, write the answers using one color pen or pencil. After four minutes, complete the remaining items with the other color pen or pencil.

Teaching the Activity

Begin this lesson by reading the vignette on the *Portfolios* Activity Page in the *Student Guide*. Review the purpose and focus of the portfolios established in your classroom in Unit 2 Lesson 5. Discuss the types of pieces and the number of pieces that students should include in their portfolios. If there are pieces that you, as the teacher, want included in the portfolio, tell students this before they begin to look through their collection folders.

Students look through the work they collected this year. They should have work in both their collection folders and their portfolio folders. Use *Question 1* in the Explore section of the *Student Guide* to help students choose appropriate items from their collection folders to add to their portfolios. After students select the pieces that they feel best show their growth, they should organize them in chronological order. *Question 2* directs students to update their Tables of Contents. *Question 3* asks students to write a paragraph comparing a piece of work they completed at the beginning of the year to one they completed recently.

Portfolios

Look at the work in your portfolios. Compare work from the beginning of the year to work you have just completed. Have you improved?

I have. I used to just write down answers. Now I show my work in lots of ways: I draw pictures, write sentences, make graphs...

I can't wait to show my portfolio to my mom and dad! They will be amazed.

Explore

1. Choose items from your collection folder to add to your portfolio. Choose items that are similar to the work that is already in your portfolio. Here are some examples of things you can choose:
   A. The *Experiment Review* from Lesson 1 of this unit.
   B. The solution to a problem you have solved. For example, you may choose to include your solutions to the problems in *The Many-Eyed Dragonfly.*
   C. A lab you have completed. *Area vs. Length* is a good example.
   D. Items your teacher recommends.

2. Add the name of each new piece to your Table of Contents. Include a short description of the work and the date it was finished.

3. Write a paragraph comparing two pieces of work in your portfolio that are alike in some way. For example, you can compare two labs or your solutions to two problems. One piece should be new, and one should be from the beginning of the year. Use these questions to help you write your paragraph:

   • Which two pieces did you choose to compare?
   • How are they alike? How are they different?
   • Do you see any improvement in the newest piece of work? Explain.
   • How could you improve your newest piece of work?

Portfolios   SG • Grade 4 • Unit 16 • Lesson 6 **439**

Student Guide - page 439

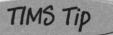

Students should have an opportunity to celebrate the accomplishments that their portfolios represent. Since this is the last opportunity students will have to share their portfolios, you may want to make time for them to present their portfolios within the classroom. One way to do this is to have students work in pairs. Each student can then present his or her portfolio to a partner. As students present the pieces they have selected, they can explain why they made the choices they did. Students can also present the one piece they feel best represents their growth this year.

Homework and Practice

- Students can share their portfolios with their parents. Encourage students to tell their parents what they can do now in mathematics that they were not able to do at the beginning of the school year.

- DPP Bit Q provides practice using convenient numbers to estimate with large numbers.

Assessment

DPP Task R is an inventory of all the division facts. Record students' fluency with the division facts on the *Observational Assessment Record*. Transfer documentation from the Unit 16 *Observational Assessment Record* to students' *Individual Assessment Record Sheets*.

At a Glance

Math Facts and Daily Practice and Problems

DPP Bit Q provides practice rounding and making estimates with large numbers. Task R is an assessment of all the division facts.

Teaching the Activity

1. Read the vignette on the *Portfolios* Activity Page in the *Student Guide*.
2. Review the focus and purpose of the portfolios established in your classroom earlier this year.
3. Provide an opportunity for students to review the work in their collection folders and their portfolio folders. Indicate any piece that you, as the teacher, want included in the portfolios.
4. Students select work to include in their final portfolios. They then update the table of contents for their portfolio.
5. Students celebrate and share their final portfolios with the rest of the class.

Homework

Students share their portfolios with their parents for homework.

Assessment

1. DPP Task R is the *Division Facts Inventory Test* and assesses fluency with the division facts. Record students' fluency with the division facts on the *Observational Assessment Record*.
2. Transfer appropriate Unit 16 observations to the *Individual Assessment Record Sheets*.

Notes:

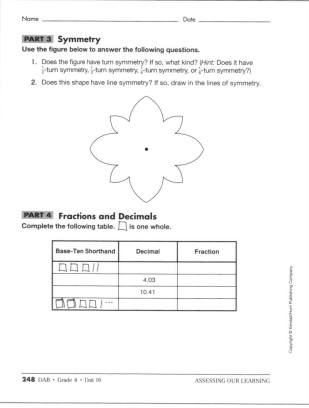

Discovery Assignment Book - page 247

Discovery Assignment Book (p. 247)

Part 2. Multiplication Tables

1.

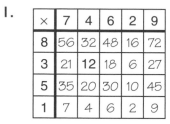

×	7	4	6	2	9
8	56	32	48	16	72
3	21	12	18	6	27
5	35	20	30	10	45
1	7	4	6	2	9

2.

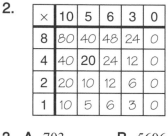

×	10	5	6	3	0
8	80	40	48	24	0
4	40	20	24	12	0
2	20	10	12	6	0
1	10	5	6	3	0

3. **A.** 703   **B.** 5606
    C. 3000   **D.** 750
    E. 46,000   **F.** 2000

Discovery Assignment Book - page 248

Discovery Assignment Book (p. 248)

Part 3. Symmetry

1. Yes, $\frac{1}{4}$-turn symmetry
2. Yes.

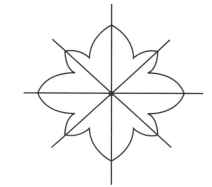

Part 4. Fractions and Decimals

Base-Ten Shorthand	Decimal	Fraction
⬜⬜⬜ //	3.2	$3\frac{2}{10}$ or $3\frac{1}{5}$
⬜⬜⬜⬜ ···	4.03	$4\frac{3}{100}$
⬜ //// ·	10.41	$10\frac{41}{100}$
⬜⬜⬜⬜ / ···	22.13	$22\frac{13}{100}$

Discovery Assignment Book (p. 249)

Part 5. School Days

Answers will vary. One possible solution is given for each question.

1. $200 \times 5 = 1000$ days
2. $250 - 180 = 70; 70 \times 5 = 350$ days
3. $200 \times 13 = 2600$ days

Part 6. Multiplication and Division Practice

A. 4928
B. 1104
C. 3920
D. 14,160
E. 125
F. 993 R2
G. 60
H. 868

Possible strategy for D: 3500×4 is 3500 doubled or 7000 and 7000 doubled again or 14,000.

Name _____ Date _____

PART 5 School Days
Use the data below to answer the following questions.

Country	Average Number of School Days
U.S.A.	180
Canada	186
England	192
Japan	243

1. About how many days will a child in England have gone to school when he or she has attended school for 5 years?

2. Yoshi lives in Japan. He has gone to school for 5 years. Jackie lives in the United States. She has gone to school for 5 years. About how many more days has Yoshi gone to school than Jackie?

3. About how many days does a student in the U.S.A. have to go to school to graduate from high school? (To graduate from high school, most students must go to school for 13 years including kindergarten.)

PART 6 Multiplication and Division Practice
Solve the following problems using paper and pencil or mental math. Show your work on a separate sheet of paper. Estimate to make sure your answers are reasonable. Explain your estimation strategy for D.

A. $64 \times 77 =$ _____
B. $23 \times 48 =$ _____
C. $70 \times 56 =$ _____
D. $3540 \times 4 =$ _____
E. $875 \div 7 =$ _____
F. $5960 \div 6 =$ _____
G. $3000 \div 50 =$ _____
H. $7812 \div 9 =$ _____

ASSESSING OUR LEARNING   DAB • Grade 4 • Unit 16 **249**

Discovery Assignment Book - page 249

Discovery Assignment Book - page 250

Discovery Assignment Book (p. 250)

Part 7. Function Machines

1. A.

Input N	Output 3 + 2 × N
1	5
2	7
3	9
4	11
5	13
6	15
7	17
8	19

B.

Input N	Output 5 × N
1	5
2	10
3	15
4	20
5	25
6	30
7	35
8	40

2. No, the outputs are not the same. If the order of operations is followed correctly in Table A, the number (N) is multiplied by 2 first, then the 3 is added.

Part 8. Downhill Racer

1.–2.

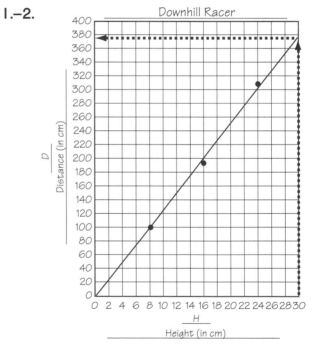

3. Answers will vary. The graph above shows $D = 375$ cm when $H = 30$. Accept answers between 340 and 410 cm.

Glossary

This glossary provides definitions of key vocabulary terms in the Grade 4 lessons. Locations of key vocabulary terms in the curriculum are included with each definition. Components Key: URG = *Unit Resource Guide* and SG = *Student Guide.*

A

Acre (URG Unit 6; SG Unit 6)
A measure of land area equal to 43,560 square feet.

Acute Angle (URG Unit 2 & Unit 9; SG Unit 2)
An angle that measures less than 90°.

All-Partials Algorithm
(URG Unit 7; SG Unit 7)
A paper-and-pencil method for solving multiplication problems. Each partial product is recorded on a separate line. (*See also* partial product.)

$$\begin{array}{r} 186 \\ \times\ 3 \\ \hline 18 \\ 240 \\ 300 \\ \hline 558 \end{array}$$

Angle (URG Unit 2; SG Unit 2)
The amount of turning or the amount of opening between two rays that have the same endpoint.

Angle of Turning (URG Unit 9)
The smallest angle through which a figure can be turned about the center of turning so that the figure coincides with itself.

Area (SG Unit 2)
The area of a shape is the amount of space it covers, measured in square units.

Array (URG Unit 4)
An array is an arrangement of elements into a rectangular pattern of (horizontal) rows and (vertical) columns.

Average (URG Unit 1 & Unit 5; SG Unit 1 & Unit 5)
A number that can be used to represent a typical value in a set of data. (*See also* mean and median.)

B

Base (of an exponent) (SG Unit 4)
When exponents are used, the number being multiplied. In $3^4 = 3 \times 3 \times 3 \times 3 = 81$, the 3 is the base and the 4 is the exponent. The 3 is multiplied by itself 4 times.

Base-Ten Board (URG Unit 3; SG Unit 3)
A tool to help children organize base-ten pieces when they are representing numbers.

Base-Ten Pieces (URG Unit 3; SG Unit 3)
A set of manipulatives used to model our number system as shown in the figure below. Note that a skinny is made of 10 bits, a flat is made of 100 bits, and a pack is made of 1000 bits.

Nickname	Picture	Shorthand
bit		•
skinny		/
flat		
pack		

Base-Ten Shorthand (URG Unit 3; SG Unit 3)
A pictorial representation of the base-ten pieces is shown in Unit 3.

Benchmarks (URG Unit 6; SG Unit 6)
Numbers convenient for comparing and ordering numbers, e.g., $0, \frac{1}{2}, 1$ are convenient benchmarks for comparing and ordering fractions.

Best-Fit Line (URG Unit 5; SG Unit 5)
The line that comes closest to the points on a point graph.

Binning Data (URG Unit 13)
Placing data from a data set with a large number of values or large range into intervals in order to more easily see patterns in the data.

Bit (URG Unit 3 & Unit 6; SG Unit 3)
A cube that measures 1 cm on each edge. It is the smallest of the base-ten pieces and is often used to represent 1. (*See also* base-ten pieces.)

C

Categorical Variable (URG Unit 1; SG Unit 1)
Variables with values that are not numbers. (*See also* variable and value.)

Center of Turning (URG Unit 9; SG Unit 9)
A point on a plane figure around which it is turned. In particular, the point about which an object with turn symmetry is rotated.

Centimeter (SG Unit 10)
A unit of length in the metric system. A centimeter is $\frac{1}{100}$ of a meter.

Certain Event (URG Unit 14; SG Unit 14)
An event that has a probability of 1 (100%).

Common Fraction (URG Unit 10)
Any fraction that is written with a numerator and denominator that are whole numbers. For example, $\frac{3}{4}$ and $\frac{9}{4}$ are both common fractions. (*See also* decimal fraction.)

Commutative Property of Multiplication
(URG Unit 3 & Unit 4)
This is also known as the Order Property of Multiplication. Changing the order of the factors does not change the product. For example, $3 \times 5 = 5 \times 3 = 15$. Using variables, $n \times m = m \times n$.

Composite Number (URG Unit 4)
A number that has more than two distinct factors. For example, 9 has three factors (1, 3, 9) so it is a composite number.

Convenient Number (URG Unit 1 & Unit 7; SG Unit 7)
A number used in computation that is close enough to give a good estimate, but is also easy to compute with mentally, e.g., 25 and 30 are convenient numbers for 27.

Cubic Centimeter (URG Unit 8; SG Unit 8)
The volume of a cube that is one centimeter long on each edge.

D

Decimal (URG Unit 3)
1. A number written using the base-ten place value system.
2. A number containing a decimal point. (*See also* decimal fraction.)

Decimal Fraction (URG Unit 10)
A fraction written as a decimal. For example, 0.75 and 0.4 are decimal fractions and $\frac{75}{100}$ and $\frac{4}{10}$ are called common fractions.

Decimeter (URG Unit 10; SG Unit 10)
A unit of length in the metric system. A decimeter is $\frac{1}{10}$ of a meter.

Degree (URG Unit 2; SG Unit 2)
A degree (°) is a unit of measure for angles. There are 360 degrees in a circle.

Denominator (URG Unit 10 & Unit 12; SG Unit 10 & Unit 12)
The number below the line in a fraction. The denominator indicates the number of equal parts in which the unit whole is divided. For example, the 5 is the denominator in the fraction $\frac{2}{5}$. In this case the unit whole is divided into five equal parts.

Dividend (URG Unit 3; SG Unit 3)
The number that is divided in a division problem, e.g., 12 is the dividend in $12 \div 3 = 4$.

Divisible (URG Unit 7; SG Unit 7)
A number a is divisible by a number b, if there is no remainder when a is divided by b. For example, 12 is divisible by 4 ($12 \div 4 = 3$), but **not** by 5 ($12 \div 5 = 2$ R2).

Division Sentence (SG Unit 3)
A number sentence involving division.

Divisor (URG Unit 3 & Unit 8; SG Unit 3 & Unit 8)
In a division problem, the number by which another number is divided. In the problem $12 \div 4 = 3$, the 4 is the divisor, the 12 is the dividend, and the 3 is the quotient.

E

Edge (URG Unit 9; SG Unit 9)
A line segment where two faces of a three-dimensional figure meet.

Equilateral Triangle (URG Unit 2 & Unit 9; SG Unit 9)
A triangle with all sides and all angles equal.

Equivalent Fractions (URG Unit 12; SG Unit 12)
Fractions that have the same value, e.g., $\frac{2}{4} = \frac{1}{2}$.

Estimate (URG Unit 3, Unit 6, & Unit 7; SG Unit 7)
1. (verb) To find *about* how many.
2. (noun) An approximate number.

Even Number (SG Unit 4)
Numbers that are multiples of 2 (2, 4, 6, 8, etc.) are called even numbers.

Exponent (URG Unit 4; SG Unit 4)
The number of times the base is multiplied by itself. In $3^4 = 3 \times 3 \times 3 \times 3 = 81$, the 3 is the base and the 4 is the exponent. The 3 is multiplied by itself 4 times.

Extrapolation (URG Unit 5; SG Unit 5)
Using patterns in data to make predictions or to estimate values that lie beyond the range of values in the set of data.

F

Face (URG Unit 9; SG Unit 9)
A plane figure that is one side of a three-dimensional figure.

Fact Family (URG Unit 3 & Unit 8; SG Unit 3 & Unit 8)
Related math facts, e.g., $3 \times 4 = 12$, $4 \times 3 = 12$, $12 \div 3 = 4$, $12 \div 4 = 3$.

Factor (URG Unit 3 & Unit 4; SG Unit 3, Unit 4, & Unit 7)
1. In a multiplication problem, the numbers that are multiplied together. In the problem $3 \times 4 = 12$, 3 and 4 are the factors.
2. Whole numbers that can be multiplied together to get a number. That is, numbers that divide a number evenly, e.g., 1, 2, 3, 4, 6, and 12 are all the factors of 12.

Factor Tree (URG Unit 4; SG Unit 4)
A diagram that shows the prime factorization of a number.

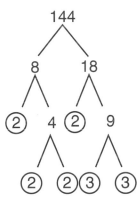

Fair Game or Fair Number Cube (URG Unit 14)
A game in which it is equally likely that any player will win. A number cube is fair if all the faces are equally likely to appear.

Fewest Pieces Rule (URG Unit 3 & Unit 10; SG Unit 3)
Using the least number of base-ten pieces to represent a number. (*See also* base-ten pieces.)

Fixed Variables (URG Unit 1, Unit 2, & Unit 5; SG Unit 5)
Variables in an experiment that are held constant or not changed.

Flat (URG Unit 3 & Unit 6; SG Unit 3)
A block that measures 1 cm $\times$ 10 cm $\times$ 10 cm. It is one of the base-ten pieces and is often used to represent 100. (*See also* base-ten pieces.)

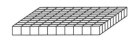

Forgiving Method of Division (URG Unit 13; SG Unit 13)
A paper-and-pencil method for division in which successive partial quotients are chosen and partial products are subtracted from the dividend, until the remainder is less than the divisor. The sum of the partial quotients is the quotient. For example, 644 ÷ 7 can be solved as shown at the right. This method of division is called the forgiving method because it "forgives" estimates of the partial quotients that are too low.

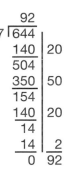

Front-End Estimation (URG Unit 3)
Estimation by looking at the left-most digit.

Function (URG Unit 15)
A rule that assigns to any input number exactly one output number. More generally, a rule that assigns to the elements of one set (the domain) exactly one element of another set (the target).

G

H

Hexagon (URG Unit 2)
A six-sided polygon.

Hieroglyphics (URG Unit 11)
An ancient Egyptian form of writing.

I

Identity Property of Multiplication (URG Unit 3)
This is also known as the Property of One for Multiplication. One times any number is that number. Using variables, $n \times 1 = n$.

Impossible Event (URG Unit 14; SG Unit 14)
An event that has a probability of 0 or 0%.

Infinite (URG Unit 9)
Cannot be counted in a finite amount of time. More than any number.

Interpolation (URG Unit 5; SG Unit 5)
Making predictions or estimating values that lie between data points in a set of data.

Intersect (SG Unit 9)
To meet or cross.

J

K

L

Likely Event (URG Unit 14; SG Unit 14)
An event that has a high probability of occurring.

Line (URG Unit 9; SG Unit 9)
A set of points that form a straight path extending infinitely in two directions.

Line Segment (URG Unit 9; SG Unit 9)
A part of a line between and including two points called the endpoints.

Line of Symmetry (URG Unit 9; SG Unit 9)
A line is a line of symmetry for a plane figure if, when the figure is folded along this line, the two parts match exactly.

Line Symmetry (URG Unit 9; SG Unit 9)
A figure has line symmetry if it has at least one line of symmetry.

Liter (SG Unit 8)
Metric unit used to measure volume. A liter is a little more than a quart.

M

Manipulated Variable (URG Unit 5 & Unit 10; SG Unit 5)
In an experiment, the variable with values known at the beginning of the experiment. The experimenter often chooses these values before data is collected. The manipulated variable is often called the independent variable.

Mass (URG Unit 8 & Unit 15; SG Unit 15)
The amount of matter in an object.

Mean (URG Unit 1 & Unit 5; SG Unit 5)
An average of a set of numbers that is found by adding the values of the data and dividing by the number of values.

Measurement Division (URG Unit 4)
Division as equal grouping. The total number of objects and the number of objects in each group are known. The number of groups is the unknown. For example, tulip bulbs come in packages of 8. If 216 bulbs are sold, how many packages are sold?

Measurement Error
The unavoidable error that occurs due to the limitations inherent to any measurement instrument.

Median (URG Unit 1 & Unit 5; SG Unit 1 & Unit 5)
For a set with an odd number of data arranged in order, it is the middle number. For an even number of data arranged in order, it is the number halfway between the two middle numbers.

Megabit (URG Unit 6)
A base-ten model that is a cube with an edge of length 100 cm. It represents 1,000,000 since it has a volume of 1,000,000 cubic cm.

Meniscus (URG Unit 8; SG Unit 8)
The curved surface formed when a liquid creeps up the side of a container (for example, a graduated cylinder).

Meter (SG Unit 10)
A unit of length in the metric system. A meter is a bit more that 39 inches.

Milliliter (ml) (URG Unit 8; SG Unit 8)
A measure of capacity in the metric system that is the volume of a cube that is one centimeter long on each side.

Millimeter (SG Unit 10)
A unit of length in the metric system. A millimeter is one-thousandth of a meter, i.e., one-tenth of a centimeter.

Millions Period (URG Unit 6; SG Unit 6)
The sequence of digits (if any) in the millions place, the ten-millions place, and the hundred millions place. In the number 12,**456,**789,987 the millions period is in bold type.

Multiple (URG Unit 4 & Unit 7; SG Unit 4 & Unit 7)
A number is a multiple of another number if it is evenly divisible by that number. For example, 12 is a multiple of 2 since 2 divides 12 evenly.

Multiplicand (URG Unit 11)
Either of the numbers being multiplied in a multiplication problem.

N

Negative Number (URG Unit 3; SG Unit 3)
A number less than zero; a number to the left of zero on a horizontal number line.

Net (URG Unit 9; SG Unit 9)
A way of representing the surface of a three-dimensional solid in two-dimensions. A net can be obtained by cutting the surface along edges until it can be laid flat on a plane.

Number Sentence
An equation or inequality with numbers. For example, $3 \times 2 + 5 = 10 + 1$ and $2 < 3 + 1$

Numeral (URG Unit 3)
A symbol used to represent a number.

Numerator (URG Unit 10 & Unit 12; SG Unit 10 & Unit 12)
The number written above the line in a fraction. For example, the 2 is the numerator in the fraction $\frac{2}{5}$. (*See also* denominator.)

Numerical Variable (URG Unit 1; SG Unit 1)
Variables with values that are numbers. (*See also* variable and value.)

O

Obtuse Angle (URG Unit 2 & Unit 9; SG Unit 2)
An angle that measures more than 90°.

Odd Number (SG Unit 4)
Numbers that are not multiples of 2 (1, 3, 5 ,7, etc.) are called odd numbers.

Ones Period (URG Unit 6; SG Unit 6)
The sequence of digits (if any) in the ones place, the tens place, and the hundreds place. In the number 12,456,789,**987** the ones period is in bold type.

Operation (SG Unit 7)
A process that takes two numbers and results in a third. This, more precisely, is called a binary operation. For example, addition, subtraction, multiplication, and division are operations.

Order of Operations (URG Unit 7; SG Unit 7)
A convention that determines how to find the value of an expression that has more than one operation.

P

Pack (URG Unit 3; SG Unit 3)
A cube that measures 10 cm on each edge. It is one of the base-ten pieces and is often used to represent 1000. (*See also* base-ten pieces.)

Papyrus (URG Unit 11)
A type of writing paper used by the ancient Egyptians.

Parallel Lines (URG Unit 9; SG Unit 9)
Lines that are in the same direction. In the plane, parallel lines are lines that do not intersect.

Parallelogram (URG Unit 9; SG Unit 9)
A quadrilateral with two pairs of parallel sides.

Partitive Division (URG Unit 4 & Unit 13)
Division as equal sharing. The total number of objects and the number of groups are known. The number of objects in each group is the unknown. For example, Frank has 144 marbles that he divides equally into 6 groups. How many marbles are in each group?

Perimeter (URG Unit 2; SG Unit 2)
The distance around a two-dimensional shape.

Period (URG Unit 6; SG Unit 6)
A group of three places in a large number, starting on the right, often separated by commas as shown at the right.

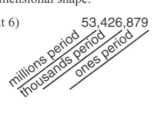

Perpendicular (URG Unit 9; SG Unit 9)
Perpendicular lines are lines that meet at right angles.

Perspective (URG Unit 9)
The art of drawing solid objects on a flat surface so that it produces the same impression as do the actual objects when viewed from a particular point.

Point (URG Unit 9)
An exact position in the plane or in space.

Polygon (URG Unit 9; SG Unit 9)
A two-dimensional connected figure made of line segments in which each endpoint of every side meets with an endpoint of exactly one other side.

Polyhedron (URG Unit 9)
A connected geometric solid whose surface is made of polygons.

Portfolio (URG Unit 2)
A collection of student work that shows how a student's skills, attitudes, and knowledge change over time.

Positive Number (URG Unit 3; SG Unit 3)
A number greater than zero; a number to the right of zero on a horizontal number line.

Powers of Two (URG Unit 6; SG Unit 6)
2 multiplied by itself a certain number of times. $2^1 = 2$, $2^2 = 2 \times 2 = 4$, $2^3 = 2 \times 2 \times 2 = 8$, etc.

Prime Factor (URG Unit 4; SG Unit 4)
A factor of a number that is itself prime.

Prime Number (URG Unit 4; SG Unit 4)
A number that has exactly two factors, itself and 1. For example, 7 has exactly two distinct factors, 1 and 7.

Prism (URG Unit 9; SG Unit 9)
A polyhedron that has two congruent faces, called bases, that are parallel to each other, and all other faces are parallelograms. If the other faces are rectangles the prism is called a right prism.

Prisms   Not a prism

Probability (URG Unit 14; SG Unit 14)
A number from 0 to 1 (0% to 100%) that describes how likely an event is to happen. The closer that the probability of an event is to one, the more likely the event will happen.

Product (URG Unit 3; SG Unit 3 & Unit 4)
The answer to a multiplication problem. In the problem $3 \times 4 = 12$, 12 is the product.

Q

Quadrilateral (URG Unit 9; SG Unit 2 & Unit 9)
A polygon with four sides. (*See also* polygon.)

Quick Paper-and-Pencil Method for Addition
   (URG Unit 3; SG Unit 3)
A traditional method for
adding multidigit numbers.
See example at right:

$$\begin{array}{r} \overset{1}{1}\overset{1}{3}26 \\ +575 \\ \hline 1901 \end{array}$$

**Quick Paper-and-Pencil Method for
   Subtraction** (SG Unit 3)
A traditional method for subtraction.
For example:

$$\begin{array}{r} \overset{0}{\cancel{1}}\overset{12}{\cancel{23}}\overset{1}{7} \\ -459 \\ \hline 778 \end{array}$$

Quotient (URG Unit 3 & Unit 13; SG Unit 3 & Unit 8)
The answer to a division problem. In the problem
$12 \div 3 = 4$, the 4 is the quotient.

R

Ray (URG Unit 9; SG Unit 9)
A part of a line that has one endpoint and extends
indefinitely in one direction.

Recording Sheet (URG Unit 3; SG Unit 3)
A place value chart used for addition and subtraction
problems.

Rectangle (URG Unit 2 & Unit 9)
A quadrilateral with four right angles.

Reflex Angle (URG Unit 2)
An angle larger than 180° but less than 360°.

Regular (URG Unit 9)
A polygon is regular if all sides are of equal length and
all angles are equal.

Remainder (URG Unit 13)
Something that remains or is left after a whole number
division problem. The portion of the dividend that is not
evenly divisible by the divisor, e.g., $16 \div 5 = 3$ with
1 as a remainder.

Responding Variable (URG Unit 5 & Unit 10;
   SG Unit 5)
The variable whose values result from the experiment.
Experimenters find the values of the responding variable
by doing the experiment. The responding variable is often
called the dependent variable.

Rhombus (URG Unit 2)
A quadrilateral with four sides of equal length.

Right Angle (URG Unit 2 & Unit 9; SG Unit 2)
An angle that measures 90°.

Roman Numeral (URG Unit 3; SG Unit 3)
A system of representing numbers used by the
Romans. The symbol I represents 1, V represents
five, X represents ten, etc.

Rounded Number (URG Unit 6 & Unit 7)
See rounding.

Rounding (URG Unit 6)
Replacing a number with the nearest convenient number.
Numbers are often rounded to the nearest whole number,
ten, hundred, fifty, etc.

S

Skinny (URG Unit 3 & Unit 6; SG Unit 3)
A block that measures 1 cm × 1 cm
× 10 cm. It is one of the base-ten
pieces that is often used to represent 10.
(*See also* base-ten pieces.)

Solid (URG Unit 9; SG Unit 9)
A three-dimensional figure that has volume greater
than 0.

Square (URG Unit 2)
A polygon with four equal sides and four right angles.

Square Inch (SG Unit 2)
The area of a square with a side length of one inch.

Square Number (URG Unit 4; SG Unit 4)
A number that is the result of multiplying a whole
number by itself. For example, 36 is a square number
since $36 = 6 \times 6$.

Square Root (URG Unit 15)
The square root of a number N is the number whose square
is N. The symbol for square root is $\sqrt{}$. For example,
the square root of 25 is 5, since $5 \times 5 = 25$. In symbols
we write $\sqrt{25} = 5$. The square root of 26 is not a whole
number.

Subtractive Principle (URG Unit 3; SG Unit 3)
A method of interpreting certain Roman numerals.
For example, IX represents 9 while XI represents 11.

Super Bit (URG Unit 6)
A base-ten model that is a cube with an edge of length
10 cm. It represents 1,000 since it has a volume of 1,000
cubic centimeters. It is usually called a pack.

Super Flat (URG Unit 6)
A base-ten model that is a rectangular solid that measures
10 cm × 100 cm × 100 cm. It represents 100,000 since
it has a volume of 100,000 cubic cm.

Super Skinny (URG Unit 6)
A base-ten model that is a rectangular solid that measures
10 cm × 10 cm × 100 cm. It represents 10,000 since it
has a volume of 10,000 cubic cm.

Survey (SG Unit 13)
An investigation conducted by collecting data from a sample of a population and then analyzing it. Usually surveys are used to make predictions about the entire population.

T

Tally
A way of recording a count by making marks. Usually tallies are grouped in fives. ‖‖‖ ‖‖‖

Ten Percent (10%) (URG Unit 6 & Unit 7)
10 out of every hundred or $\frac{1}{10}$.

Thousands Period (URG Unit 6; SG Unit 6)
The sequence of digits (if any) in the thousands place, the ten-thousands place, and the hundred-thousands place. In the number 12,456,**789,**987 the thousands period is in bold type.

TIMS Laboratory Method (URG Unit 1; SG Unit 1)
A method that students use to organize experiments and investigations. It involves four phases: draw, collect, graph, and explore. It is a way to help students learn about the scientific method.

Translational Symmetry (URG Unit 9)
A pattern has translational symmetry if there is a translation that moves the pattern so it coincides with itself.

Trapezoid (URG Unit 2)
A quadrilateral with exactly one pair of parallel sides.

Triangle (URG Unit 2)
A polygon with three sides.

Turn-Around Facts (URG Unit 3; SG Unit 3)
Multiplication facts that have the same factors but in a different order, e.g., $3 \times 4 = 12$ and $4 \times 3 = 12$. (*See also* commutative property of multiplication.)

Turn-Around Rule (URG Unit 4)
A term used to describe the commutative property of multiplication. (*See also* commutative property of multiplication.)

Turn Symmetry (URG Unit 9; SG Unit 9)
A figure has turn symmetry if it can be rotated around a point (called the center of turning) through an angle less than 360° and so that the turned figure matches the original.

Type of Turn Symmetry (URG Unit 9)
The number of times a figure coincides with itself when it is rotated about its center of turning. For example, a square has 4-fold turn symmetry. This is also called $\frac{1}{4}$ turn symmetry.

U

Undefined (Division by Zero) (URG Unit 13; SG Unit 13)
We say division by 0 is undefined because there is no number that satisfies the definition of division when 0 is the divisor. For example, if there were a number $N = 3 \div 0$, it would be the unique number N that makes $N \times 0 = 3$ a true statement. There is no such N.

Unlikely Event (URG Unit 14; SG Unit 14)
An event that has small probability.

V

Value (URG Unit 1; SG Unit 1)
The possible outcomes of a variable. For example, red, green, and blue are possible values for the variable *color*. Two meters and 1.65 meters are possible values for the variable *length*.

Variable (URG Unit 1; SG Unit 1)
1. An attribute or quantity that changes or varies. (*See also* categorical variable and numerical variable.)
2. A symbol that can stand for a variable.

Vertex (URG Unit 2 & Unit 9; SG Unit 2 & Unit 9)
The common endpoint of two rays or line segments.

Volume (URG Unit 8 & Unit 9; SG Unit 8)
The measure of the amount of space occupied by an object.

Volume by Displacement (SG Unit 8)
A way of measuring volume by measuring the amount of water (or some other fluid) it displaces.

W

Weight (URG Unit 15; SG Unit 15)
A measure of the pull of gravity on an object. One unit for measuring weight is the pound.

X

Y

Z

Zero Property of Multiplication (URG Unit 3)
Any number times zero is zero. Using variables, $n \times 0 = 0$.